JAMESTOWN  EDUCATION

The Outer Edge™
Still Unsolved

Henry Billings
Melissa Billings

 Glencoe

New York, New York   Columbus, Ohio   Chicago, Illinois   Peoria, Illinois   Woodland Hills, California

Reviewers

Kati Pearson
Literacy Coordinator
Carver Middle School
4500 West Columbia Street
Orlando, FL 32811

Suzanne Zweig
Reading Specialist
Sullivan High School
6631 North Bosworth Avenue
Chicago, IL 60626

Beth Dalton
Reading Consultant
Los Angeles County Office
　of Education
9300 Imperial Avenue
Downey, CA 90240

Susan Jones
Reading Specialist
Alief Hastings High School
12301 High Star
Houston, Texas 77072

Glencoe

The **McGraw-Hill** Companies

ISBN: 0-07-869052-8

Send all queries to:
McGraw-Hill Companies
190 E. Randolph Street Suite 400
Chicago, IL 60601

8 9 10   QVS   15 14 13

Contents

Unit Three

To the Student

Just about everybody is interested in unsolved mysteries. Whether the mystery is about a person who has disappeared, or a strange creature who is frightening a town, or a terrible sickness that is killing thousands of people, we all identify with the fear of the unknown. There are 13 true stories in this book. In them you will learn about some chilling mysteries. Some of them are old. Some of them are new. All of them are still unsolved.

As you do the lessons in this book, you will improve your reading skills. This will help you increase your reading comprehension. You will also improve your thinking skills. The lessons include types of questions often found on state and national tests. Working with these questions will help you prepare for tests you may have to take in the future.

How to Use This Book

About the Book. *Still Unsolved* has three units. Each one has four lessons. Each lesson starts with a true story. The stories are about strange events in the past that have never been explained and are still unsolved today. Each story is followed by a group of seven exercises. They test comprehension and thinking skills. They will help you understand and think about what you read. At the end of the lesson, you can give your personal response. You can also rate how well you understood what you read.

The Sample Lesson The first lesson in the book is a sample. It explains how to complete the questions. It also shows how to score your answers. The correct answers are printed in lighter type. In some cases, the reasons an answer is correct are given. Studying these reasons will help you learn how to think through the questions. You might have questions about how to do the exercises or score them. If so, you should ask those questions now, before you start Unit One.

Working Through Each Lesson. Start each lesson by looking at the photo. Next read the caption. Before you read the story, guess what you think it will be about. Then read the story.

After you finish the story, do the exercises. Study the directions for each exercise. They will tell you how to mark your answers. Do all seven exercises. Then check your work. Your teacher will give you an answer key to do this. Follow the directions after each exercise to find your score. At the end of the lesson, add up your total score. Record that score on the graph on page 115.

At the end of each unit, you will complete a Compare and Contrast Chart. The chart will help you see what some of the stories in that unit have in common. It will also help you explore your own ideas about the events in the stories.

Sample Lesson

MARFA'S MYSTERY LIGHTS
VIEWING AREA
1 MILE

Strange Lights over Texas

MARFA'S MYSTERY LIGHTS
VIEWING AREA
· 1 MILE ·

Marfa, Texas, is a quiet little town. During the day, it seems like any other town in West Texas. But just wait until the sun goes down. That's when things get spooky. Something strange happens here at night. No one knows why. And no one knows how. But it's been going on for more than 100 years.

2 About an hour after the sun sets, lights appear in the sky. They always show up in the same place. They are not right over the town. They are off to the south. But they can be seen for miles around.

3 Nothing about these lights makes sense. One minute their light is soft, but the next minute it is bright. The lights don't come out every night. In fact, there is no way to know when they will show up. The time of year doesn't matter. Neither does the weather. They come on clear nights and cloudy nights. They come when it's hot and when it's cool. They come when the air is still. They come when the wind is blowing. They even come in the pouring rain.

Shown here is a roadside sign along a highway in Marfa, Texas. It directs tourists to a viewing area where they can see the strange lights that appear in the sky over Marfa.

4 Sometimes these lights seem to hang in the air. Sometimes they spin or dive. They dance from spot to spot. They flash on and off. Sometimes one light breaks into two. At times they seem to be headed straight toward Marfa. At other times they seem to be running away. The lights also change colors. They may be white. They may be red. They may be green, pink, blue, or yellow.

5 They are called the Ghost Lights of Marfa. Some people think they really are the work of a ghost. Back in the 1860s, an Apache Indian chief was killed near Marfa. Some people say his ghost lives on. They say the lights come from his ghost as it wanders through the night. "Nobody's been able to say it isn't so," says Alma Cabezuela.

6 That may be. But most people don't believe in ghosts. So they have to look for answers somewhere else. If a ghost isn't behind the lights, then what is?

7 Some people think the lights come from cars. There are roads near the place where the lights appear. But there is a problem with this answer. The lights have been seen since the 1880s. That was long before the first car came to Texas.

8 Could the lights be from fires? Robert Ellison thought they could be. Ellison was the first person to talk openly about the lights. He saw them one night in 1883.

He was taking care of his cows at the time. Ellison tried to chase the lights on his horse. He couldn't catch them. Later he wondered whether the lights had come from campfires. He talked to people who lived in Marfa. It turned out that they had been seeing the lights for years. They, too, had thought of fires. They had even gone out and looked around. But they had never found any sign of fire.

9 One answer might be that the lights are made by gas. That makes sense. A certain kind of gas sometimes comes from rotting plants. As the gas floats up toward the sky, it can blow up. It can turn into balls of fire. But no gas has been found where the lights appear.

10 Could there be something strange about the air in Marfa? That's what some people think. They believe there might be some air pocket here that is bending moonlight back toward Earth. That sounds good. But no one has been able to find this air pocket.

11 Scientists are no help. They keep coming to Marfa. They bring special tools. They take pictures of the sky. They watch the lights for weeks at a time. Still, they have found no answer. They agree that the lights are real. But they don't know what makes them.

12 That is okay with most people in Marfa. They like having a mystery in town. After all, they aren't afraid of the lights. "These lights are mild," says the mayor of the town. "They are friendly. They're not going to hurt anybody."

13 Some people do find the lights scary. But they also think the lights are fun. One man tells how he saw the lights while flying his plane on a dark night. "You haven't lived until you have seen the Marfa lights," he says. "That will make the hair on the back of your neck curl."

14 People come from around the world to see the lights. That brings a lot of money into the town. Maybe that's why people in Marfa like the lights so much. "I have no idea what the lights are," says Marfa's Connie Brisbin. "And, like most people in town, we don't want to know. We're just glad they're here."

15 Another woman in town agrees. "The Marfa lights are a mystery," she says. "Let them stay a mystery."

A Finding the Main Idea

One statement below tells the main idea of the article. One statement is too general, or too broad. The other statement explains only part of the article; it is too narrow. Label the statements using the following key:

M—Main Idea   B—Too Broad   N—Too Narrow

____N____ 1. In 1883 Robert Ellison got on his horse and chased the strange lights near Marfa, Texas, but he never found out what made them. [This statement is true, but it is *too narrow*. It gives only a few facts from the article.]

____B____ 2. At night it is fun to look up into the sky. When people see a light in the sky, they often wonder where it is coming from. [This statement is *too broad*. It does not tell anything about the lights in Marfa, Texas.]

____M____ 3. Strange lights dance in the sky near Marfa, Texas. For many years, people have been trying to figure out where the lights come from. [This statement is the *main idea*. It tells you that the article is about the puzzling lights over Marfa, Texas.]

Score 4 points for each correct answer.

_____ **Total Score:** Finding the Main Idea

B Recalling Facts

How well do you remember the facts in the article? Put an X in the box next to the answer that correctly completes each statement.

1. The lights over Marfa, Texas,

☒ a. appear about one hour after the sun sets.
☐ b. appear only when there are no clouds in the sky.
☐ c. look the same every time.

2. People call the lights the Ghost Lights of Marfa because

☐ a. the lights make pictures of people from the town who have died.
☒ b. they think that the lights come from the ghost of an Indian chief who was killed near Marfa.
☐ c. the lights appear only after someone has died.

3. The first person who openly said he saw the lights was

☐ a. an Apache Indian chief in the 1860s.
☐ b. Robert Ellison in 1953.
☒ c. Robert Ellison in 1883.

4. Most people in Marfa

☐ a. have been hurt by the lights at one time or another.
☒ b. like the mystery lights.
☐ c. want to find a way to get rid of the lights.

Score 4 points for each correct answer.

_____ **Total Score:** Recalling Facts

C | Making Inferences

When you draw a conclusion that is not directly stated in the text, you are making an inference. Put an X in the box next to the statement that is a correct inference.

1.

☒ a. People might not be as interested in Marfa if it weren't for the lights.

☐ b. Each year, people in Marfa probably put out a list of the days when people can see the lights.

☐ c. The lights over Marfa are probably what made people start the town long ago.

2.

☐ a. The night sky around Marfa is always bright with big city lights.

☐ b. Everyone in Marfa goes to big parties whenever the lights come out.

☒ c. Some people probably think the Marfa lights are exciting.

Score 4 points for each correct answer.

_____ **Total Score:** Making Inferences

D | Using Words

Put an X in the box next to the definition below that is closest in meaning to the underlined word.

1. Some people say that ghosts live in that spooky old house.

☐ a. friendly

☒ b. scary

☐ c. pretty

2. If ghosts appear, I'll shout "boo" and scare them away.

☒ a. show up

☐ b. go away

☐ c. see

3. The families were told not to put their campfires too close to their tents.

☐ a. fires made indoors for cooking

☐ b. big fires that cannot be stopped

☒ c. small fires made by people who camp

4. The wood in the floor was rotting, so when my sister jumped on the floor, she fell through.

☒ a. falling apart

☐ b. new and strong

☐ c. painted

5. I don't understand how the TV works. It is a <u>mystery</u> to me.

☐ a. something that looks silly
☒ b. something that cannot be explained
☐ c. something that seems too good to be true

6. With his <u>mild</u> way of talking, the man slowly made friends with the puppy.

☐ a. wild
☐ b. angry
☒ c. kind

Score 4 points for each correct answer.

_____ **Total Score:** Using Words

E | Author's Approach

Put an X in the box next to the correct answer.

1. What is the author's purpose in writing this article?

☐ a. to teach the reader about the Apache people
☒ b. to tell the reader about something that cannot be explained
☐ c. to describe what happens when gas floats up into the sky

2. From the statements below, choose the one that you believe the author would agree with.

☒ a. It would be interesting to see the lights over Marfa.
☐ b. To be safe, you should stay away from Marfa on nights when the lights appear.
☐ c. The story of the lights over Marfa was made up by the people who live in the town.

3. Some people say that the lights come from cars. Choose the statement below that best explains how the author deals with the opposite point of view.

☐ a. The author points out that no one around Marfa drives a car, yet the lights can still be seen.
☐ b. The author points out that gas can come from things that are rotting and that gas can blow up.
☒ c. The author points out that the lights could be seen before there were cars around Marfa.

Score 4 points for each correct answer.

_____ **Total Score:** Author's Approach

F	**Summarizing and Paraphrasing**

Put an X in the box next to the correct answer.

1. Which summary says all the important things?

☐ a. The lights that come out at night over Marfa, Texas, change colors. They can be bright or soft. [This summary gives some small details from the article but misses too many important ones.]

☐ b. Scientists have come to look at the lights over Marfa, Texas. They say that the lights are real. [This summary gives some small details from the article but misses too many important ones.]

☒ c. For over 100 years, people in Marfa, Texas, have seen lights just south of town. There are many ideas to explain where the lights come from. But no one knows for sure. [This summary says all the most important things.]

2. Which sentence means the same thing as the following sentence? "Seeing the Marfa lights will make the hair on the back of your neck curl."

☐ a. When you see the Marfa lights, you will get curly hair.

☐ b. Seeing the Marfa lights can make you feel sick.

☒ c. Seeing the Marfa lights will shock you. [When you say that something makes the hair on the back of your neck curl, it means that it surprises or shocks you.]

Score 4 points for each correct answer.

_____ **Total Score:** Summarizing and Paraphrasing

G	**Critical Thinking**

Put an X in the box next to the correct answer.

1. Choose the statement below that states a fact.

☐ a. The Marfa lights are beautiful.

☒ b. The Marfa lights show up south of the town.

☐ c. Scientists should be able to find out what makes the lights.

2. The Marfa lights and lights from cars are alike because

☐ a. they both change colors.

☐ b. they both have been seen outside Marfa since the 1880s.

☒ c. they both appear near the same place.

3. Which paragraphs provide information that supports your answer to question 2?

☐ a. paragraphs 1 and 2

☒ b. paragraphs 2 and 7

☐ c. paragraphs 5 and 6

4. What is the effect of the lights over Marfa?

☒ a. They make Marfa different from other West Texas towns.

☐ b. They make everyone who lives in Marfa very afraid.

☐ c. They stop people from going near Marfa.

5. How is the story of the Marfa lights an example of something that is still unsolved?

☐ a. No one knows which Apache chief was killed near Marfa.

☒ b. No one knows what makes the lights.

☐ c. No one knows what time of day the lights will appear.

Score 4 points for each correct answer.

_____ **Total Score:** Critical Thinking

Enter your score for each activity. Add the scores together. Record your total score on the graph on page 115.

_____ Finding the Main Idea

_____ Recalling Facts

_____ Making Inferences

_____ Using Words

_____ Author's Approach

_____ Summarizing and Paraphrasing

_____ Critical Thinking

_____ **Total Score**

Personal Response

What was most surprising or interesting to you about this article? [In your own words, write down one interesting fact that you learned from the article.]

_____

_____

Self-Assessment

A word or phrase in the article that I do not understand is

_____

_____

[Choose one word or phrase that gave you trouble as you read the article. Write it here.]

Self-Assessment

You can take charge of your own progress. Here are some features to help you focus on your progress in learning reading and thinking skills.

Personal Response and Self-Assessment. These questions help you connect the stories to your life. They help you think about your understanding of what you have read.

Comprehension and Critical Thinking Progress Graph. A graph at the end of the book helps you to keep track of your progress. Check the graph often with your teacher. Together, decide whether you need more work on some skills. What types of skills cause you trouble? Talk with your teacher about ways to work on these.

A sample Progress Graph is shown on the right. The first three lessons have been filled in to show you how to use the graph.

Comprehension and Critical Thinking Progress Graph

Directions: Write your score for each lesson in the box under the number of the lesson. Then put a small X on the line directly above the number of the lesson and across from the score you earned. Chart your progress by drawing a line to connect the Xs.

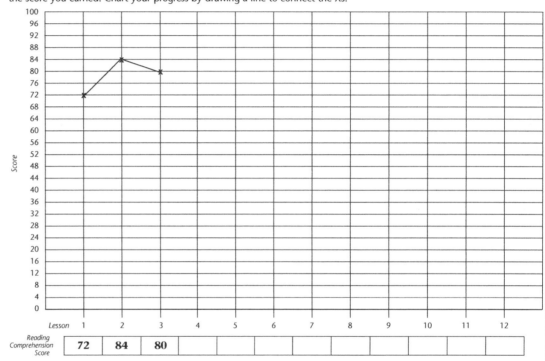

Lesson	1	2	3	4	5	6	7	8	9	10	11	12
Reading Comprehension Score	72	84	80									

UNIT ONE

The Lost Dutchman's Mine

Would you like to be rich—really rich? If your answer is yes, here's what you need to do. Go to Arizona. Head east from Phoenix, toward the Superstition Mountains. In these hills there is a gold mine. It is called the Lost Dutchman's Mine. Some people say it is the richest mine in the world. If you find it, the gold inside could be yours.

2 Doesn't that sound good? But don't pack your bags just yet. There is some bad news. People have looked for this mine for many years. No one has been able to find it. Some people have lost all their money looking for it. Others have lost their lives.

3 The story of the mine begins with Jacob Waltz. Sometime around 1840, he moved from Europe to the United States. No one knows the year for sure. There are other things about Waltz that are not definite. But we do know he lived in California. He spent a long time looking for gold there. He didn't have much luck. So in 1863 Waltz moved to Arizona.

4 When he got there, Waltz went on looking for gold. For 10 years he found nothing. But one day his luck changed—or so the story goes. It is said that Waltz was in a bar with his friend Jacob Weisner when a fight broke out. Waltz and Weisner stopped the fight. They saved the life of a young Mexican named Miguel Peralta. The Peralta family wanted to thank them. So the Peraltas told Waltz and Weisner about a secret gold mine. It wasn't just any old mine. It turned out to have more gold in it than Waltz or Weisner could believe.

5 The two men began to work the mine. But one day, Apache Indians appeared. They killed Weisner. We don't know why. But it scared Jacob Waltz. He left the mountains and went to live in Phoenix. First, though, he covered up the entrance to the mine. He made sure no one else would see it.

6 For a long time, Waltz told no one about the mine. From time to time he did sneak back to it, but he only dug up enough gold to live on for a while.

7 In Phoenix, Waltz bought a small farm and raised chickens. He became friends with a woman who ran a store. Her name was Julia Thomas. In 1891 Thomas ran short of money. It looked as if she might lose her store. Waltz wanted to help. He told Thomas about the mine.

Shown here is the Weaver's Needle, a peak in the Superstition Mountains of Arizona. The Lost Dutchman's Mine might be hidden in this area.

Until then, Thomas had thought of Waltz as a poor chicken farmer. But now Waltz pulled out a piece of gold and showed it to her. "There's a great deal more where that came from," he said.

8 Waltz promised to take Thomas to the mine. They made plans to go. But by this time, Waltz was an old man. Before they could leave, he became sick and died.

9 Waltz died without telling anyone where the mine was. But he left behind some clues. Just before he died, Waltz wrote, "No miner will ever find my mine." Then he added, "To find my mine you must pass a cow barn. It can't be seen from the trail, but I can see the trail from my mine." Waltz threw in a few more clues as well. Here are two of them:

10 "If you pass three red hills, you have gone too far."

11 "Across from the mine is a cave."

12 It wasn't much to go on. But that didn't stop people from trying to find the mine. Over the years, thousands of gold hunters have gone to the Superstition Mountains. The first person to go was Julia Thomas herself. After a few weeks, she gave up. She needed money, so she printed and sold maps to the Lost Dutchman's Mine. She did not know where it was, of course. Still, people bought her maps.

13 The story of the mine spread around the world. People rushed to Arizona. They all hoped to find the mine. Many spent years looking. But none found it. Some went broke, and some ended up dead.

14 Dr. Adolph Ruth is one of those who lost their lives looking for the Lost Dutchman's Mine. Ruth set out in 1931. No one knows what happened. But somewhere in the mountains, he was killed. His head was cut off. Another person died while looking for the mine 16 years later. This time the man's name was James Cravey. Many other men have died mysterious deaths in these same mountains. Has someone been trying to keep people from finding the mine? Or are the deaths accidental?

15 No one knows. In fact, we still don't know whether the Lost Dutchman's Mine is real. As time has passed, people have made up their own clues. Lies have been mixed in with the truth. It has grown harder and harder to tell which is which. But as one man says, "Don't let the truth stand in the way of a good story." So if you're looking to get rich quick, you might want to make that trip to Arizona after all.

A | Finding the Main Idea

One statement below tells the main idea of the article. One statement is too general, or too broad. The other statement explains only part of the article; it is too narrow. Label the statements using the following key:

M—Main Idea   **B—Too Broad**   **N—Too Narrow**

_____ 1. Finding a gold mine could make you rich for the rest of your life.

_____ 2. Jacob Waltz promised to take Julia Thomas to his gold mine in the Superstition Mountains, but he died before they could make the trip.

_____ 3. People have been looking for the Lost Dutchman's gold mine in the Superstition Mountains for many years with no luck.

Score 4 points for each correct answer.

_____ **Total Score:** Finding the Main Idea

B | Recalling Facts

How well do you remember the facts in the article? Put an X in the box next to the answer that correctly completes each statement.

1. Jacob Waltz met Miguel Peralta in

☐ a. Europe.
☐ b. California.
☐ c. Arizona.

2. The Peralta family told Waltz where a gold mine was because they

☐ a. could not get to the mine themselves but wanted someone to have the gold there.
☐ b. wanted to thank him for saving Miguel's life.
☐ c. owed him a lot of money but couldn't pay him.

3. Waltz left his mine just after

☐ a. Apache Indians killed his friend.
☐ b. he found out that there was no more gold in the mine.
☐ c. he grew very old and sick.

4. In 1931 Dr. Adolph Ruth

☐ a. found Waltz's gold mine.
☐ b. told people that Waltz never really had a gold mine.
☐ c. was killed while trying to find Waltz's mine.

Score 4 points for each correct answer.

_____ **Total Score:** Recalling Facts

C | Making Inferences

When you draw a conclusion that is not directly stated in the text, you are making an inference. Put an X in the box next to the statement that is a correct inference.

1.

☐ a. People don't take chances that might hurt them, no matter how much money they could make.

☐ b. Some people will take big chances to get rich.

☐ c. Nobody really cares much about getting rich.

2.

☐ a. Julia Thomas was a clever woman who knew how to make money.

☐ b. Julia Thomas never believed that Waltz had a gold mine.

☐ c. Jacob Waltz's clues to finding his mine are clear and easy to follow.

Score 4 points for each correct answer.

_____ **Total Score:** Making Inferences

D | Using Words

Put an X in the box next to the definition below that is closest in meaning to the underlined word.

1. She wanted a <u>definite</u> answer to her question.

☐ a. wrong

☐ b. silly

☐ c. certain

2. A table blocked the <u>entrance</u>, so no one could come into the store before it opened.

☐ a. the way to get into a place

☐ b. the way to leave a place

☐ c. the cost of getting into a place

3. The little girl tried to <u>sneak</u> away after she took the last cookie from the jar.

☐ a. move in a loud way, making a lot of noise

☐ b. move in a quiet way, as if in secret

☐ c. move in a silly way, trying to make people laugh

4. The lucky <u>miner</u> wanted to keep all the gold he found under the ground for himself.

☐ a. a worker who digs things out of the earth

☐ b. a worker who writes stories and poems

☐ c. someone who tries to do the right thing

5. Because no one knows what the words on the cave wall mean, they seem <u>mysterious</u>.

☐ a. wrong

☐ b. true

☐ c. hard to explain

6. The way I dress may look <u>accidental</u>, but I choose my clothes with great care.

☐ a. done by chance

☐ b. done many times

☐ c. planned ahead of time

Score 4 points for each correct answer.

_____ **Total Score:** Using Words

E | Author's Approach

Put an X in the box next to the correct answer.

1. The main purpose of the first paragraph is to

☐ a. let the reader know that the Lost Dutchman's Mine might not be real.

☐ b. tell the reader that this story is about a lost gold mine.

☐ c. tell how Jacob Waltz got the gold mine from the Peralta family.

2. Choose the statement below that is the weakest argument for looking for the Lost Dutchman's Mine.

☐ a. You could die looking for it.

☐ b. If you find it, you will be rich.

☐ c. Looking for the gold mine may make you tired and sick.

3. The author probably wrote this article in order to

☐ a. get readers to look for their own gold mines in Arizona.

☐ b. make readers angry with Jacob Waltz for leaving such bad clues.

☐ c. tell an interesting story.

Score 4 points for each correct answer.

_____ **Total Score:** Author's Approach

F | Summarizing and Paraphrasing

Put an X in the box next to the correct answer.

1. Which summary says all the important things about the article?

- ☐ a. The owner of the Lost Dutchman's Mine in Arizona, Jacob Waltz, said it held a great deal of gold. He died before telling anyone where it was. People still follow clues he left as they look for the mine.

- ☐ b. Some people have died while looking for a mine in Arizona. For example, Dr. Adolph Ruth looked for it and was found with his head cut off.

- ☐ c. Julia Thomas, who ran a store in Phoenix, was a friend of a man from Europe named Jacob Waltz. She sold maps to his gold mine, but she never found it herself.

2. Which sentence means the same thing as the following sentence? "In 1891 Thomas ran short of money."

- ☐ a. Thomas won a short race that paid her a lot of money in 1891.

- ☐ b. In 1891 Thomas made a great deal of money.

- ☐ c. In 1891 Thomas did not have enough money to pay her bills.

Score 4 points for each correct answer.

_____ **Total Score:** Summarizing and Paraphrasing

G | Critical Thinking

Put an X in the box next to the correct answer.

1. Choose the statement below that states an opinion.

- ☐ a. People should not waste their time looking for the Lost Dutchman's Mine.

- ☐ b. Julia Thomas ran a store in Phoenix.

- ☐ c. The Superstition Mountains are in Arizona, east of Phoenix.

2. From information in the article, you can predict that

- ☐ a. no one still wants to find the Lost Dutchman's Mine.

- ☐ b. people will keep looking for the Lost Dutchman's Mine for many years.

- ☐ c. very soon everyone will forget all about the Lost Dutchman's Mine.

3. Dr. Adolph Ruth and James Cravey are alike because they both

- ☐ a. knew Jacob Waltz and learned about the mine from him.

- ☐ b. came from Europe.

- ☐ c. died while looking for the Lost Dutchman's Mine.

4. What was the effect of the Apaches' coming to the Lost Dutchman's Mine?

- ☐ a. People from all over the world started looking for the mine.

- ☐ b. Waltz got scared and closed up the mine.

- ☐ c. Julia Thomas started selling maps to the mine.

5. Which paragraph provides information that supports your answer to question 4?

☐ a. paragraph 4

☐ b. paragraph 7

☐ c. paragraph 5

Score 4 points for each correct answer.

_____ **Total Score:** Critical Thinking

Enter your score for each activity. Add the scores together. Record your total score on the graph on page 115.

_____ Finding the Main Idea

_____ Recalling Facts

_____ Making Inferences

_____ Using Words

_____ Author's Approach

_____ Summarizing and Paraphrasing

_____ Critical Thinking

_____ **Total Score**

Personal Response

A question I would like Jacob Waltz to answer is "_____

_____?"

Self-Assessment

When reading the article, I was having trouble with

_____

_____

The Missing Divers

It was going to be a great day. The four Canadians felt sure of that. On November 4, 1994, they gathered in Florida. They had come to fish and dive in the Gulf of Mexico. Jeff Wandich had a boat. So he and Kent Munro, Omar Shearer, and Dave Madott set out on the boat. They planned to be back by dark. But they did not make it. In fact, only one of the men ever made it back.

2 About 60 miles out, Jeff stopped the boat. From here, they could dive 129 feet down. They could get to an old ship that lay at the bottom of the ocean. The water was getting rough. The waves were more than three feet high. But the men weren't worried. They had dived in bad weather before. They put on diving suits and broke into pairs. Jeff dived with Dave, and Omar dived with Kent.

3 By the time they were finished diving, something was wrong with the boat. It was filling with water. The men couldn't save it. They jumped into the water and

Shown here are the three Canadian divers who disappeared in the Gulf of Mexico. A Web site has been set up about these divers at www.vanished.org.

hung onto a rope, hoping someone would come along and save them. No one did. Four hours later, at 7 P.M., their boat sank.

4 The men knew they were in trouble. Still, they tried to think clearly. There was a light tower about four miles away. They could see its lights flashing on and off. If they could swim to it, they could save themselves.

5 Omar wasn't sure he could make it. He didn't think he could swim that far.

6 "Omar, we don't have a choice," Dave told him. "We'll make it. We'll all make it."

7 With those brave words, the four friends began swimming.

8 "We just plugged along," Jeff later said, "side by side, with me on one end and Dave on the other, Omar and Kent between us."

9 After five minutes, Jeff felt fear washing over him. "I had tears in my eyes," he later said. He turned away so his friends would not see him cry. He swam away from them for a minute to pull himself together.

10 "I wasn't far away from them," he said, "maybe 10 feet, two waves away, and then I took a look to my left." Jeff didn't see them anymore. They were gone.

11 Jeff couldn't believe it. Where could they be? He called to them and thought he heard them answer.

But he could not see them. By this time, the waves were about four feet high. He thought the waves were keeping him from seeing them. In any case, he knew they were all headed for the light tower. So he turned toward it and began swimming again.

12   For the next four hours, Jeff swam through the waves and the wind. He tried not to think about sharks. He was exhausted. But he kept swimming. At last he reached the tower. He climbed up onto it, hoping his friends might already be there. They weren't. Jeff thought they would come soon. As the hours passed, he thought a boat must have saved them. At last, after 35 hours on the tower, he was picked up by the Coast Guard. That's when he learned that his friends were still missing.

13   The Coast Guard looked all over for Omar, Kent, and Dave. They used planes and boats. They used their best tools. It was one of the biggest searches ever in the Gulf of Mexico. It covered 23,000 square miles of sea. But no bodies were found. After six days, the Coast Guard gave up.

14   The families of the missing men did not want to give up. They promised $300,000 to anyone who would help them find the men. They gave people money just to keep looking. But it did no good. Omar Shearer, Dave Madott, and Kent Munro were gone.

15   How could this be? The water was warm. The men were young and strong, and they all knew how to swim. None of them had been sick or hurt, and they were all wearing special clothes to help them float. So it does not seem likely they all drowned. Even if they did, their bodies would have floated. Surely the Coast Guard would have found one of these floating bodies.

16   Did sharks devour the men? Scientists say no. There were not many sharks in this part of the ocean. There were some. But they weren't the kind that goes after people. Besides, sharks wouldn't eat the men's special diving clothes. So pieces of these clothes should have been found.

17   Was Jeff lying? Did he kill his friends or lie about what happened to them? That is hard to believe because he loved these men. They had been friends for years. And to prove that he was telling the truth, he took a lie detector test. This test tells whether someone is lying. "The kid passed with flying colors," said one man. "He was telling the truth."

18   Some people think a boat picked up Kent, Omar, and Dave. Many people sneak through the Gulf of Mexico to buy and sell drugs. Did one of these people kill the men? Or kidnap them? Or give them a lift? Did the three men run off and start lives in some other country?

19   Years later, we still don't know what happened. The families of the missing men keep hoping for answers. But none has been found. The question is still there: What happened to Kent Munro, Omar Shearer, and Dave Madott?

A | Finding the Main Idea

One statement below tells the main idea of the article. One statement is too general, or too broad. The other statement explains only part of the article; it is too narrow. Label the statements using the following key:

M—Main Idea   B—Too Broad   N—Too Narrow

_____ 1. Jeff Wandich took four hours to swim to a light tower after his boat sank in the Gulf of Mexico.

_____ 2. When their boat sank in the Gulf of Mexico, four divers tried to swim to a light tower. Only one made it. The others are missing.

_____ 3. Four men found out that diving was harder than they thought it would be when they took their boat out in the Gulf of Mexico.

Score 4 points for each correct answer.

_____ **Total Score:** Finding the Main Idea

B | Recalling Facts

How well do you remember the facts in the article? Put an X in the box next to the answer that correctly completes each statement.

1. The four men went diving so they could

☐ a. look at an old ship on the ocean floor.
☐ b. get a good look at fish and other sea animals.
☐ c. find something they had lost.

2. After their boat sank, the men tried to swim to a

☐ a. big ship that was passing by.
☐ b. town by the ocean.
☐ c. light tower they could see.

3. Jeff went away from his friends so they would

☐ a. not see him cry.
☐ b. leave him in the ocean alone.
☐ c. think he was dead.

4. The families of the missing men offered

☐ a. $300,000 to anyone who could help find them.
☐ b. $200,000 to anyone who could help find them.
☐ c. $100,000 to anyone who could help find them.

Score 4 points for each correct answer.

_____ **Total Score:** Recalling Facts

C | Making Inferences

When you draw a conclusion that is not directly stated in the text, you are making an inference. Put an X in the box next to the statement that is a correct inference.

1.

☐ a. Jeff did not really care what the other divers thought of him.

☐ b. The Coast Guard keeps looking until missing people are found.

☐ c. Swimming in a sea with four-foot waves is very hard.

2.

☐ a. The men were probably tired even before their boat sank.

☐ b. The men thought that swimming to the light tower would be fun.

☐ c. It would have been easier for the friends to swim to land instead of to the light tower.

Score 4 points for each correct answer.

_____ **Total Score:** Making Inferences

D | Using Words

Put an X in the box next to the definition below that is closest in meaning to the underlined word or phrase.

1. Standing at the top of the <u>tower</u>, you could see the whole town below you.

☐ a. a building that is short and wide

☐ b. a building that is tall but not wide

☐ c. the part of a building that is below the ground

2. I had a <u>choice</u>: I could stay at home and watch TV, or I could go to the game.

☐ a. the right to choose

☐ b. a problem

☐ c. a funny story

3. Carrying a heavy sack of potatoes, the farmer <u>plugged</u> along on the road to town.

☐ a. ate

☐ b. danced

☐ c. kept doing something

4. People hoped their friends had not <u>drowned</u> when the big ship sank.

☐ a. made it to shore

☐ b. died under water

☐ c. seen something beautiful

5. Doug was so hungry that he was able to <u>devour</u> the sandwich in just a few minutes.

☐ a. put in a box
☐ b. cut up into pieces
☐ c. eat quickly

6. Lee worried that a stranger might <u>kidnap</u> her puppy, so she always kept it locked up in the backyard.

☐ a. take away someone who does not want to go
☐ b. be kind to someone or something
☐ c. give someone a present

Score 4 points for each correct answer.

_____ **Total Score:** Using Words

E | Author's Approach

Put an X in the box next to the correct answer.

1. What is the author's purpose in writing this article?

☐ a. to get the reader to learn to swim
☐ b. to tell the reader about something puzzling
☐ c. to explain why no one should go diving alone

2. From the statements below, choose the one that you believe the author would agree with.

☐ a. It is hard to understand how three strong men could go missing so quickly.
☐ b. All the men knew that Jeff's boat would probably sink, even before they started their dive.
☐ c. Trying to swim to the light tower was probably a bad idea.

3. Choose the statement below that best describes the author's opinion in paragraph 16.

☐ a. It is a good thing that the men wore special diving clothes.
☐ b. Scientists do not know much about sharks.
☐ c. Sharks probably didn't eat the men.

Score 4 points for each correct answer.

_____ **Total Score:** Author's Approach

F | Summarizing and Paraphrasing

Put an X in the box next to the correct answer.

1. Which summary says all the important things about the article?

☐ a. Three friends—Kent Munro, Omar Shearer, and Dave Madott—went swimming in the Gulf of Mexico. They are now missing. Their families are sad and still wonder what happened to them.

☐ b. Four men were diving in the Gulf of Mexico when their boat sank. They began to swim. One of them went off alone for a minute, and when he came back the others were gone. Only he was saved. People looked for the others, but no one knows what happened to them.

☐ c. Four men were swimming toward a light tower in the Gulf of Mexico. The light tower was four miles from the place where they had been diving. When one of them got to the tower, he held on for 35 hours. Then he was saved.

2. Which sentence means the same thing as the following sentence? "The kid passed with flying colors."

☐ a. The young man did not do as well as he had hoped.

☐ b. The young man did poorly.

☐ c. The young man did very well.

Score 4 points for each correct answer.

_____ **Total Score:** Summarizing and Paraphrasing

G | Critical Thinking

Put an X in the box next to the correct answer.

1. Choose the statement below that states a fact.

☐ a. Jeff should never have left his friends in the ocean.

☐ b. Jeff spent 35 hours alone at the light tower.

☐ c. Jeff should not have gone diving with his friends.

2. From information in the article, you can predict that

☐ a. Jeff will soon admit that he made up the whole story.

☐ b. the families of the missing men will always wonder what happened to them.

☐ c. no one will be allowed to go diving in the Gulf of Mexico again.

3. Jeff Wandich and his friends are different because

☐ a. only Jeff had a boat.

☐ b. Jeff stayed on the boat while his friends went diving.

☐ c. only Jeff had dived in bad weather before.

4. What was the effect of the boat's sinking?

☐ a. The divers knew they had to swim to the tower to save themselves.

☐ b. The waves grew to about four feet high.

☐ c. The friends had to put on diving suits and break into pairs.

5. Which lesson about life does this story teach?

☐ a. Nothing can stop someone who is trying hard.

☐ b. Things don't always turn out as we plan them.

☐ c. If you plan things well, they are sure to turn out fine.

Score 4 points for each correct answer.

_____ **Total Score:** Critical Thinking

Enter your score for each activity. Add the scores together. Record your total score on the graph on page 115.

_____ Finding the Main Idea

_____ Recalling Facts

_____ Making Inferences

_____ Using Words

_____ Author's Approach

_____ Summarizing and Paraphrasing

_____ Critical Thinking

_____ **Total Score**

Personal Response

How do you think Jeff felt when the Coast Guard stopped looking for his friends? _____

_____

_____

Self-Assessment

I can't really understand how _____

_____

Death by Anthrax

THE POLICE NEED YOUR HELP

Kathy Nguyen

Vietnamese Name "Xihn Thi Nguyen"

Height: 5 feet tall   Weight: ~ 120 pounds

On Sunday October 28, 2001, Kathy Nguyen entered Lenox Hill Hospital complaining of stomach pain and shortness of breath. She passed away on October 31, 2001. The cause of death has been attributed to inhalation anthrax.

The FBI, NYPD, NYC – Department of Health still need more information. Anyone who saw her or knows of her movements and activities between October 11, 2001 and October 28, 2001 please call:

Task Force Hotline: 646 259-8539
                    212 384-8309
                    646 259-8497

Something was wrong. Kathy Nguyen (new–win) felt terrible. She was cold. She was tired. Every part of her body hurt. And she could not stop coughing. For two days the 61-year-old Nguyen tried to keep going. She showed up for work at the Manhattan Eye, Ear and Throat Hospital in New York. But by the third day, her heart was racing. She found it hard to breathe. At last, she asked a friend to take her to a hospital.

2   Doctors thought there might be a problem with Nguyen's heart. But tests showed that was not true. After three days, doctors found out what was really wrong. But by then it was too late. The next day, Kathy Nguyen died. A disease called anthrax had killed her.

3   A disease is a sickness. The anthrax disease is caused by bacteria. People get sick if they even touch anthrax bacteria. They get sick if they breathe in the bacteria. These bacteria are rare. Most of us never come near them. But in the fall of 2001, when Nguyen died, they were a big problem. That's because someone was using them to kill people.

The poster on this column shows a picture of Kathy Nguyen, who died from anthrax. Police put it up hoping someone might know how Nguyen got the anthrax.

4   Nguyen's death came just a few weeks after September 11, 2001. On that day, terrorists had killed thousands of people in the United States. Terrorists are people who frighten or hurt others to get their way. Now a new terrorist was at work. He or she was sending anthrax letters through the mail. These letters were filled with bacteria. They gave people anthrax. Sixteen people got sick. Three had died.

5   In each case, police knew what had happened. Some of the sick people were mail workers. The letters had passed through their hands at work. The rest were people who had opened the letters. Either way, it was clear how they got the disease.

6   Nguyen was a different story. She was not a mail worker. And she had not gotten an anthrax letter. So how did Nguyen get sick? That was the question. Quickly, police went to work to find the answer.

7   They brought in scientists to test Nguyen's home. There were no anthrax bacteria in it. Next they checked the hospital where she had worked. Nguyen had worked in a room where lots of things were stored. Scientists checked the whole room. They found no anthrax bacteria. They ran tests throughout the hospital. Nothing.

8   They went to the place where Nguyen got her mail. An anthrax letter might have come through there.

Bacteria from an anthrax letter could have stuck to a piece of Nguyen's mail. This, too, turned out to be a dead end. None of the bacteria showed up at Nguyen's mail center.

9 Now police were really worried. Had the killer found some new way to spread anthrax? If so, the police had to find it. That was the only way to keep people safe.

10 Doctors said the bacteria had entered Nguyen's body a few days before she got sick. So police tried to find out what she had done during that time. Where had she gone? How had she spent her time? They talked with Nguyen's neighbors. These neighbors all said the same thing. Kathy Nguyen led a very quiet life. She had lived next to them for 10 years. She had always been friendly and kind. But she had not gone out much. On Sundays she went to a church up the street. And during the week she went to work. That was about it.

11 "It's not like Kathy traveled a lot or visited a lot of people," said one woman.

12 A second neighbor agreed. "She was always from her job to her house, from her job to her house. She sometimes said she was tired from working all the time and just wanted to be home."

13 This was not much help. Still, the police did their best. They checked every place they could think of where she might have been. They checked the stores where she shopped. They checked the place where she washed her clothes. They found out that she had a favorite restaurant. They checked it out. They even found out what subway line she took to work. They checked each stop between her home and her job.

14 They didn't come up with a thing.

15 In the end, the police gave up. So did the scientists. They just could not find out where Kathy Nguyen had picked up anthrax.

16 For a while, not knowing how Nguyen had gotten sick made everyone pretty worried. "It's very scary," said one of Nguyen's friends, "because what happened to her could happen to anyone."

17 That was true. But Americans were lucky. After Nguyen died, only a few more people came down with anthrax. By the end of 2001, the scare was ending. Police still did not know who had sent the anthrax letters. More puzzling, they did not know how Kathy Nguyen got the disease. Maybe someday they will find the answer. For now, though, her case is still unsolved. 🎗

A | Finding the Main Idea

One statement below tells the main idea of the article. One statement is too general, or too broad. The other statement explains only part of the article; it is too narrow. Label the statements using the following key:

M—Main Idea   B—Too Broad   N—Too Narrow

_____ 1. In 2001 Kathy Nguyen died of a rare disease called anthrax, and no one knows how she got it.

_____ 2. Kathy Nguyen worked at the Manhattan Eye, Ear and Throat Hospital in New York before she died of a rare disease.

_____ 3. Bacteria can cause many diseases that can make people sick or even kill them.

Score 4 points for each correct answer.

_____ **Total Score:** Finding the Main Idea

B | Recalling Facts

How well do you remember the facts in the article? Put an X in the box next to the answer that correctly completes each statement.

1. When Kathy Nguyen got sick, she

☐ a. got a bad stomachache and could not keep food down.
☐ b. felt her heart racing, could not stop coughing, and found it hard to breathe.
☐ c. was very weak, could not see straight, and had trouble hearing.

2. In 2001 mail workers got anthrax when someone

☐ a. sent anthrax bacteria in letters.
☐ b. put bacteria into the workers' water.
☐ c. put bacteria into the workers' food.

3. Neighbors said that Kathy Nguyen

☐ a. liked to travel and had just come back from another country.
☐ b. was always having loud parties at her home.
☐ c. was a quiet person who did not go many places.

4. According to the article, scientists looked for anthrax bacteria in all of these places <u>except</u>

☐ a. in Nguyen's father's home.
☐ b. at a restaurant Nguyen liked.
☐ c. at Nguyen's home.

Score 4 points for each correct answer.

_____ **Total Score:** Recalling Facts

C | Making Inferences

When you draw a conclusion that is not directly stated in the text, you are making an inference. Put an X in the box next to the statement that is a correct inference.

1.

☐ a. Kathy Nguyen probably thought she had anthrax even before she got to the hospital.

☐ b. After you touch or breathe in anthrax bacteria, a few days can pass before you die.

☐ c. None of Kathy Nguyen's neighbors knew her at all.

2.

☐ a. If you have anthrax, you spread it to everyone who comes near you.

☐ b. Anyone who gets anthrax is sure to die of the disease.

☐ c. If you have a cough, it doesn't always mean that you have anthrax.

Score 4 points for each correct answer.

_____ **Total Score:** Making Inferences

D | Using Words

Put an X in the box next to the definition below that is closest in meaning to the underlined word.

1. If you <u>breathe</u> slowly and deeply, you will soon feel better.

☐ a. look from side to side

☐ b. put one foot in front of the other

☐ c. take air in and let it out

2. Thousands of <u>bacteria</u> swim in a drop of water, but they are too small to be seen.

☐ a. very tiny living things

☐ b. pieces of dirt

☐ c. weeds

3. Because that frog is <u>rare</u>, most people don't know what it looks like.

☐ a. seen all the time

☐ b. hardly ever seen

☐ c. beautiful

4. Three people were killed in the <u>deadly</u> car crash.

☐ a. angry

☐ b. not too bad

☐ c. able to kill

5. We got off the <u>subway</u> and walked up the stairs to the street.

☐ a. a train that travels underground
☐ b. a train that travels above ground
☐ c. a train that makes no stops until the end of the line

6. The police work hard on every <u>unsolved</u> case until they find an answer.

☐ a. easy to understand
☐ b. not explained
☐ c. not important

Score 4 points for each correct answer.

_____ **Total Score:** Using Words

E | Author's Approach

Put an X in the box next to the correct answer.

1. The main purpose of the first paragraph is to

☐ a. tell where Kathy Nguyen worked.
☐ b. tell how sick Kathy Nguyen felt.
☐ c. tell Kathy Nguyen's age.

2. Choose the statement below that best describes the author's opinion in paragraph 17.

☐ a. The police stopped looking too quickly for the person who had sent the anthrax letters.
☐ b. Americans don't care anymore who sent the anthrax letters or how Kathy Nguyen got the disease.
☐ c. It was good that only a few more Americans came down with anthrax.

3. The author probably wrote this article in order to

☐ a. teach doctors how to spot anthrax.
☐ b. show how hard the police work.
☐ c. tell an interesting but sad story.

Score 4 points for each correct answer.

_____ **Total Score:** Author's Approach

F | Summarizing and Paraphrasing

Put an X in the box next to the correct answer.

1. Which summary says all the important things about the article?

☐ a. In 2001 Kathy Nguyen felt very sick, but she went to work anyway. When she felt too sick to go on, she asked a friend to take her to the hospital. She died there a few days later.

☐ b. Anthrax is a disease that is caused by bacteria. If a person touches or breathes in the bacteria, he or she can get very sick. Kathy Nguyen died of anthrax in 2001. Other Americans died of the disease that year too.

☐ c. Kathy Nguyen died of a disease called anthrax in 2001, around the same time that anthrax bacteria had shown up in the mail. Scientists looked for the way she caught the disease, but they never found it.

2. Which is the best paraphrase for the following sentence? "This, too, turned out to be a dead end."

☐ a. This did not lead anywhere either.

☐ b. This turned out to be what killed her.

☐ c. This, too, was harder than they thought it would be.

Score 4 points for each correct answer.

_____ **Total Score:** Summarizing and Paraphrasing

G | Critical Thinking

Put an X in the box next to the correct answer.

1. Choose the statement below that states an opinion.

☐ a. Police looked for anthrax bacteria at every stop along the subway line that Kathy Nguyen took to work.

☐ b. Touching or breathing in anthrax bacteria can make people come down with anthrax.

☐ c. It is sad that the doctors didn't know right away that Kathy Nguyen had anthrax.

2. Kathy Nguyen and other Americans who got anthrax in 2001 are different because

☐ a. police knew that the others got anthrax from letters.

☐ b. no one but Kathy Nguyen died of anthrax.

☐ c. only Kathy Nguyen had felt sick when she got anthrax.

3. What was the cause of scientists' going to the place where Kathy Nguyen got her mail?

☐ a. They were looking for names of people in her family so they could tell them that she died.

☐ b. They wanted to see if she had many bills to pay.

☐ c. They were looking for a letter with anthrax bacteria.

4. In which paragraph did you find the information or details to answer question 3?

☐ a. paragraph 7

☐ b. paragraph 8

☐ c. paragraph 10

5. How is the story of Kathy Nguyen's death an example of something that is still unsolved?

☐ a. No one knows which disease killed her.

☐ b. No one knows how she got anthrax.

☐ c. No one knows how anthrax is spread.

Score 4 points for each correct answer.

_____ **Total Score:** Critical Thinking

Enter your score for each activity. Add the scores together. Record your total score on the graph on page 115.

_____ Finding the Main Idea

_____ Recalling Facts

_____ Making Inferences

_____ Using Words

_____ Author's Approach

_____ Summarizing and Paraphrasing

_____ Critical Thinking

_____ **Total Score**

Personal Response

What new question do you have about this topic?

_____

_____

Self-Assessment

A word or phrase in the article that I do not understand is

_____

_____

Costa Rica's Strange Spheres

The forests of Costa Rica held a secret. But for hundreds of years, no one knew it. People thought these forests were nothing but jungle. They thought the jungle only had trees, vines, and animals. In fact, the forests did have these things. But they had something else too. They held within them one of the biggest mysteries of all time.

2   The mystery came to light in the 1930s. That's when a fruit organization went to Costa Rica. It planned to plant banana trees. First, though, it had to clear some land. So workers burned large patches of the jungle. When they did, they came across something strange. They found spheres of stone lying on the forest floor. Some of these balls were small, the size of baseballs. Others were very big. They were as big as cars. All of them looked perfectly round, and all were smooth and shiny.

3   There were hundreds of these spheres. Many were lying in bunches of 10 or more. These had been set down in a special way. Some were in lines. Some had been put together to make shapes. Some had been set on piles of dirt.

4   There was no way to tell how old the balls were. Some scientists said 400 years. Some said 10,000 years. The best guess was that they were between 1,000 and 2,000 years old. That was the age of pots and other things found nearby.

5   The people who made these balls have long since died away. They left few clues about who they were or how they lived. But one thing is clear. They must have worked very hard to make the stone balls. These people did not have great tools. Yet somehow they knew how to cut beautiful spheres out of stone. Even the biggest balls were well shaped. Scientists measured them. Each one was almost perfectly round.

6   The bigger balls were heavy. They were more than 30,000 pounds. So they must have been cut from very large blocks of stone. The blocks did not come from the jungle. This kind of rock was only found in certain spots. The nearest spot was 50 miles away. No one knows how or why the balls were moved so far.

7   Were the balls cut by hand? If so, it would have taken many years to finish each one. So maybe early Costa Rican people found an easier way. Perhaps they placed blocks of stone at the bottom of a cascade.

Shown here in front of the National Museum in San Jose, Costa Rica, are some of the strange stone balls that workers found when they went to clear some land in the Costa Rican jungle.

Water would have pounded the blocks day and night. In time, the water might have worn blocks down into balls.

8   Or maybe they used fire. They could have built a fire on a block of stone. Then they could have splashed cold water on it. Heating and cooling rock this way can help break it down. Of course, there would still have been lots of work to do. People would have had to hammer or rub each ball until it was smooth and round.

9   In any case, the people who made the balls clearly had great skill. Yet they did not use this skill to make anything else with stone. They left behind no large stone buildings. They left no other cut stones at all. Why not? Why did they spend so much time making balls and nothing else?

10   That raises the most puzzling question of all. Why did people make the balls in the first place? No one knows. Some scientists think the balls were used to point out stars. Some say the balls were placed to show where the sun rose and set at different times of year. One story is that the balls marked spots where gold could be found. And some say the balls were kept by people to show how successful they were. This last idea may sound funny. But it makes some sense. Rich people could have had workers make the stone spheres for them. The richest people would have had the biggest ones.

11   There are other ideas too. The balls might have been used for farming somehow. They might have been part of some church. They might have been works of art.

12   Could it be that the balls weren't made by people at all? Could they have come shooting out of a volcano? Could they have been made by ice during an ice age? During an ice age, ice and snow cover much of Earth. Most scientists say no. They point out that no volcano has ever tossed out stone balls. And ice did not cover Costa Rica in the last ice age. So it seems that people did make the balls. We just don't know how or why.

13   Most of the balls found so far have now been moved out of the jungle. Many have been broken. People thought there might be something inside. So they cut them up. There may be more balls hidden in Costa Rica's jungle. Maybe someday they will be found. Even so, we may never learn the secrets behind these strange stone balls. 🎗

A | Finding the Main Idea

One statement below tells the main idea of the article. One statement is too general, or too broad. The other statement explains only part of the article; it is too narrow. Label the statements using the following key:

M—Main Idea   B—Too Broad   N—Too Narrow

_____ 1. We cannot always know how the people of long ago lived or how and why they made the things they made.

_____ 2. Almost perfectly round stone balls were found in the jungle in Costa Rica. No one knows who made them or why they were made.

_____ 3. If the stone balls found in Costa Rica were made by hand, it would have taken many years to finish each one.

Score 4 points for each correct answer.

_____ **Total Score:** Finding the Main Idea

B | Recalling Facts

How well do you remember the facts in the article? Put an X in the box next to the answer that correctly completes each statement.

1. In the 1930s an organization cleared land in Costa Rica to

☐ a. make room for houses for the workers.
☐ b. make a place to plant bananas.
☐ c. make room to build a factory.

2. The biggest stone balls found in Costa Rica weigh about

☐ a. 30,000 pounds.
☐ b. 3,000 pounds.
☐ c. 300 pounds.

3. The blocks of stone that the balls were cut from could have come from

☐ a. about a mile from where the balls were found.
☐ b. about 1,000 miles from where the balls were found.
☐ c. about 50 miles from where the balls were found.

4. The people who made the stone balls

☐ a. also made beautiful buildings that are still there.
☐ b. left behind no big stone buildings.
☐ c. left behind a book that no one knows how to read.

Score 4 points for each correct answer.

_____ **Total Score:** Recalling Facts

C | Making Inferences

When you draw a conclusion that is not directly stated in the text, you are making an inference. Put an X in the box next to the statement that is a correct inference.

1.

☐ a. If people made the stones, they had no way to move very heavy things.

☐ b. The balls were important to the people who made them.

☐ c. Scientists can always tell exactly when a thing was made.

2.

☐ a. If people made the stones, they were willing to take time to make them right.

☐ b. Today, almost anyone would find it easy to make stone balls like the ones found in Costa Rica.

☐ c. The people who made the stone balls were not as smart as people are today.

Score 4 points for each correct answer.

_____ **Total Score:** Making Inferences

D | Using Words

Put an X in the box next to the definition below that is closest in meaning to the underlined word.

1. Red and yellow birds sat on the branches of trees in the hot <u>jungle</u>.

☐ a. a cold, windy place covered with ice and snow

☐ b. hot, dry land on which nothing grows

☐ c. land covered with trees and other plants

2. My father got a job with an <u>organization</u> that makes machine parts.

☐ a. building in which things are stored

☐ b. a place where people work together

☐ c. a test done to see whether something works right

3. The shape of a marble is a perfect <u>sphere</u>.

☐ a. a round body

☐ b. a small circle

☐ c. a box

4. The sound of the <u>cascade</u> travels a long way in the quiet forest.

☐ a. a place where the water in a river drops a long way

☐ b. a place where water comes up out of the ground

☐ c. a large body of quiet water, such as a lake or a pond

5. If I were <u>successful</u>, I would live in a big house, wear beautiful clothes, and drive a fine car.

☐ a. poor
☐ b. rich
☐ c. sad

6. This park is filled with rocks from a <u>volcano</u> that blew up many years ago.

☐ a. a huge ocean wave that may hurt or kill people when it comes onto land
☐ b. a storm in which the winds are high and a large amount of rain falls
☐ c. a place where the earth opens up and melted rock is thrown out

---

Score 4 points for each correct answer.

_____ **Total Score:** Using Words

| E | **Author's Approach** |

Put an X in the box next to the correct answer.

1. The author uses the first sentence of the article to

☐ a. explain how the stone balls were made.
☐ b. tell who found the stone balls.
☐ c. make the reader wonder what the secret is.

2. From the statements below, choose the one that you believe the author would agree with.

☐ a. Most people would think the stone balls are wonderful.
☐ b. Making the stone balls was a silly thing to do.
☐ c. Hardly anyone would be interested in the stone balls today.

3. The author probably wrote this article in order to

☐ a. make readers angry that some stone balls were broken.
☐ b. teach readers something they didn't know before.
☐ c. find out whether any readers know how the stone balls were made.

Score 4 points for each correct answer.

_____ **Total Score:** Author's Approach

F | Summarizing and Paraphrasing

Put an X in the box next to the correct answer.

1. Which summary says all the important things about the article?

- [ ] a. Some scientists think that the stones of Costa Rica were made by a volcano. Other think that they were left in Costa Rica by ice during an ice age. Or maybe people put big rocks under a cascade and let the water wear the rocks down into round shapes.

- [ ] b. The round stones of Costa Rica are almost perfectly round. The people who made them probably used simple tools and might have worked for years to make each one.

- [ ] c. Round stones found in the jungles of Costa Rica are a mystery. They were made long ago and are almost perfectly round. No one knows who made them or how and why they were made.

2. Which sentence means the same thing as the following sentence? "The mystery came to light in the 1930s."

- [ ] a. People found out about the mystery during the 1930s.

- [ ] b. The mystery moved closer to the sun in the 1930s.

- [ ] c. People solved the mystery during the 1930s.

Score 4 points for each correct answer.

_____ **Total Score:** Summarizing and Paraphrasing

G | Critical Thinking

Put an X in the box next to the correct answer.

1. Choose the statement below that states a fact.

- [ ] a. People should take good care of the stone balls found in Costa Rica.

- [ ] b. The stone balls were found in the jungle in Costa Rica.

- [ ] c. The stone balls are stranger than anything else that has ever been found in the world.

2. From information in the article, you can predict that

- [ ] a. scientists will break all the stone balls apart to see what is inside them.

- [ ] b. scientists will keep looking for clues about who made the stone balls and why they made them.

- [ ] c. the stone balls will all suddenly fall apart because they are no longer covered by trees and vines.

3. Putting rocks under cascades and heating and cooling rocks are alike because

- [ ] a. scientists know that both were used to make the stone balls in Costa Rica.

- [ ] b. both make rocks stronger.

- [ ] c. both can change the size or shape of rocks.

4. Which paragraphs provide information that supports your answer to question 3?

- [ ] a. paragraphs 5 and 6
- [ ] b. paragraphs 7 and 8
- [ ] c. paragraphs 9 and 10

5. How are the stone balls of Costa Rica examples of something that is still unsolved?

☐ a. No one knows who made the stone balls or why they made them.

☐ b. It is still a mystery how the stone balls were found.

☐ c. What kind of rock the balls are made from is still not known.

Score 4 points for each correct answer.

_____ **Total Score:** Critical Thinking

Enter your score for each activity. Add the scores together. Record your total score on the graph on page 115.

_____ Finding the Main Idea

_____ Recalling Facts

_____ Making Inferences

_____ Using Words

_____ Author's Approach

_____ Summarizing and Paraphrasing

_____ Critical Thinking

_____ **Total Score**

Personal Response

Would you tell other students to read this article? Explain.

_____

_____

Self-Assessment

I can't really understand how _____

_____

Compare and Contrast

Pick two articles in Unit One that tell about a mystery. Use information from the articles to fill in this chart.

Title	What is the mystery in the story?	What have people done to try to solve the mystery?	Why is the mystery still not solved?

Which of these mysteries is more interesting to you? Why? _____

_____

_____

UNIT TWO

The Mysteries of the Maya

No one knows how they did it. The Maya did not have metal tools. They did not have wheels. Yet they built fine cities with wide streets and big open parks. They put up huge temples with stones that fit together perfectly. And that was not all they did. Although they lived more than 1,000 years ago, the Maya did all kinds of things that would be amazing even today. Why, then, did the Mayan people suddenly disappear?

2   The Maya lived in parts of Mexico and Central America. They were good farmers. They knew how to drain low, wet land. They built raised fields where they could plant crops. They cut flat steps into the sides of hills to grow even more crops. And again, they did all this without metal tools.

3   The Maya were great artists. They made wonderful pots, rugs, and necklaces. They wrote books. But perhaps their biggest talent lay in math and science. The Maya studied the sky carefully. They tracked the movement of the stars, the planets, the moon, and the sun. They knew when the sun would be right overhead.

The ruins shown here are all that is left of one Mayan city. A Mayan pyramid can be seen in the top right corner of the picture.

They knew when one heavenly body would hide another from view. They figured out when Venus would rise in the evening, when it would rise in the morning, and when it would not be seen in the sky.

4   The Maya used this information to make calendars. Their calendars were outstanding. They went forward and backward in time for half a million years. The Maya had 17 calendars in all. These kept track of all the things they saw happening in the sky. The Maya used a special number system to help them. Our own system is based on the number 10. Theirs was based on the number 20.

5   And there was one more thing. The Maya knew a great deal about how sound travels. They built a huge open room called the Ball Court. This room was almost 180 feet long. Yet a whisper in one end could be heard clearly at the other end. Today's scientists don't know how the Maya were able to build such a thing.

6   With all their talents, it is no wonder the Maya built such a strong society. What is surprising is that it all came to a screeching halt. In A.D. 800 the Maya seemed to be at the top of their power. But then something happened. The Maya stopped building. They stopped planting crops. They left their cities. By about 900 the Maya were gone. All they left behind were the ruins of their once-great cities.

7　No one knows for sure what happened. Some experts think there was fighting between the rich and the poor. A few Mayan leaders were very rich. But most Mayan people were quite poor. The poor people did all the work. Perhaps they got sick of it. They might have killed the leaders. They might have driven the leaders away. Or they might have moved out of the cities themselves. That would have left the leaders with no workers. Any of these things would explain why the Mayan cities suddenly became deserted.

8　Some experts think that war caused the fall of the Maya. It is possible that the great Mayan cities began to fight each other. Wars may have wiped out most of the people. Experts have found clues to back up this idea. They have found burn marks on buildings. They have found weapons. They have also found pictures drawn by the Maya showing people at war.

9　Perhaps lack of rain killed off the Maya. By the 800s the Maya had cut down or burned almost all of their trees. They needed the land for farming. But without trees, much of the soil washed away. It flowed into lakes and ponds. Over time, the lakes and ponds filled in and dried up. Of course, the Maya still needed water. So they collected water each time it rained and then stored it. But dry weather would have been a problem. Without rain, the cities would have run out of water. In that case, the Mayan people would have had no choice. They would have had to leave the cities in search of fresh water.

10　Or maybe there were just too many people in these cities. Experts believe Mayan cities were very crowded. There may not have been enough food. People may have grown weak. Disease could have spread easily. Bones of Mayan children have been found in the ruins. These bones show the children were smaller than they should have been. So hunger and disease may have wiped out the Mayan cities.

11　Perhaps all of these things played a role in the fall of the Maya. We just don't know—and we may never find out. It may be that the mysteries of the Maya will always be with us. George Stuart puts it best. Stuart is an expert on the Maya. He says, "I wake up almost every morning thinking how little we know about the Maya."

A | Finding the Main Idea

One statement below tells the main idea of the article. One statement is too general, or too broad. The other statement explains only part of the article; it is too narrow. Label the statements using the following key:

M—Main Idea   B—Too Broad   N—Too Narrow

_____ 1. The Mayan people studied the movements of the things they saw in the sky. Their amazing calendars showed dates a half a million years in the past and in the future.

_____ 2. Long ago the Maya of Mexico and Central America were wonderful builders, farmers, scientists, and artists. How they did what they did and why they died out so suddenly are mysteries.

_____ 3. People might never be able to solve the mysteries of the Mayan people who lived in Mexico and Central America about 1,000 years ago, no matter how hard they try.

Score 4 points for each correct answer.

_____ **Total Score:** Finding the Main Idea

B | Recalling Facts

How well do you remember the facts in the article? Put an X in the box next to the answer that correctly completes each statement.

1. The Maya used what they learned about the things they saw in the sky to
   - ☐ a. make calendars.
   - ☐ b. make beautiful rugs.
   - ☐ c. drain their fields so they could plant crops.

2. The Mayan number system was based on the number
   - ☐ a. 10.
   - ☐ b. 12.
   - ☐ c. 20.

3. The small bones of Mayan children suggest that
   - ☐ a. Mayan families didn't have enough to eat.
   - ☐ b. the Mayan people went to war often.
   - ☐ c. the Mayan leaders were very rich.

4. Experts say that the Mayan cities
   - ☐ a. have never been found.
   - ☐ b. were very crowded.
   - ☐ c. were quite small.

Score 4 points for each correct answer.

_____ **Total Score:** Recalling Facts

C | Making Inferences

When you draw a conclusion that is not directly stated in the text, you are making an inference. Put an X in the box next to the statement that is a correct inference.

1.

☐ a. Most people today believe that metal tools make building things easier.

☐ b. The Maya did not often look into the skies at night.

☐ c. At the top of their power, the Maya were really only interested in relaxing and having fun.

2.

☐ a. The Maya left behind books that explain why they fell.

☐ b. Scientists have ways of figuring out when a building was built.

☐ c. The Maya thought that Earth was the only planet that goes around the sun.

Score 4 points for each correct answer.

_____ **Total Score:** Making Inferences

D | Using Words

Put an X in the box next to the definition below that is closest in meaning to the underlined word.

1. On special days, people left gifts for their gods inside and outside the huge stone temples.

☐ a. streets where people buy and sell food

☐ b. small houses where people live

☐ c. holy places where people pray

2. You need a telescope to look at heavenly bodies such as the sun, the moon, the planets, and the stars.

☐ a. having to do with the sea

☐ b. having to do with the sky

☐ c. having to do with science

3. All of these calendars show that Sunday is the first day of the week.

☐ a. pictures of events that happened long ago

☐ b. lists of names of the people in a certain group

☐ c. charts that show the days, weeks, and months of a year

4. Leonard got a special award for doing an outstanding job.

☐ a. ordinary

☐ b. wonderful

☐ c. all right

5. We must all work together to build a kind and fair <u>society</u>.

☐ a. a way of life for people
☐ b. a house in which many families live
☐ c. a party to celebrate a special event

6. All the soldiers carried their own <u>weapons</u> into battle.

☐ a. things used for writing
☐ b. things used for fighting
☐ c. things that help people hear better

Score 4 points for each correct answer.

_____ **Total Score:** Using Words

E | Author's Approach

Put an X in the box next to the correct answer.

1. What is the author's purpose in writing this article?

☐ a. to get readers to make their own calendars
☐ b. to tell readers about an interesting mystery
☐ c. to describe what happens when people don't have enough to eat

2. From the statements below, choose the one that you believe the author would agree with.

☐ a. The Maya went to war more often than most people do.
☐ b. Hardly anyone really cares what happened to the Maya.
☐ c. The Maya were a smart and hard-working people.

3. Choose the statement below that best describes the author's opinion in paragraph 3.

☐ a. The most amazing thing about the Maya was their skill in making pots.
☐ b. What is most amazing about the Maya was their understanding of math and science.
☐ c. The Maya are best known for their beautiful rugs and necklaces.

Score 4 points for each correct answer.

_____ **Total Score:** Author's Approach

F | Summarizing and Paraphrasing

Put an X in the box next to the correct answer.

1. Which summary says all the important things?

☐ a. It is a mystery how the Maya of Mexico and Central America built such great cities and learned so much math, science, and art. And no one knows why the society suddenly fell apart around A.D. 900.

☐ b. The Mayan people, who lived in Mexico and Central America, built beautiful cities without using metal tools. They were also able to drain wet fields and grow crops on the sides of mountains. They even knew about the movements of planets.

☐ c. Experts cannot agree why the Mayan people suddenly disappeared. Some say that the people rose up against their leaders. Others say that the Maya went to war. Some say that the Maya moved away from their cities because they were hungry.

2. Which sentence means the same thing as the following sentence? "Perhaps all of these things played a role in the fall of the Maya."

☐ a. Maybe all these things add to the Mayan mystery.

☐ b. Maybe all of these things worked together to make the Maya fall.

☐ c. All these things explain how the Maya became great.

Score 4 points for each correct answer.

_____ **Total Score:** Summarizing and Paraphrasing

G | Critical Thinking

Put an X in the box next to the correct answer.

1. Choose the statement below that states an opinion.

☐ a. The Maya stopped making buildings shortly after A.D. 800.

☐ b. People should not waste their time trying to figure out what happened to the Maya.

☐ c. The Maya had 17 different calendars.

2. The Mayan leaders and their people were different because

☐ a. the leaders were rich and most of the people were poor.

☐ b. the leaders worked hard while most of the people didn't work at all.

☐ c. the leaders lived in cities and most of the people lived on farms.

3. Some scientists think that the Maya cut down almost all their trees. What was the effect of cutting down the trees?

☐ a. The Mayan cities became very crowded.

☐ b. The Maya had to go to war.

☐ c. Much of the good soil washed away.

4. In which paragraph did you find the information or details to answer question 3?

☐ a. paragraph 7

☐ b. paragraph 9

☐ c. paragraph 10

5. How is the story of the Maya an example of an unsolved mystery?

☐ a. No one knows what crops the Mayan farmers planted in their fields.

☐ b. No one knows who the leaders of the Maya were.

☐ c. No one knows what made the Mayan society fall so suddenly.

Score 4 points for each correct answer.

_____ **Total Score:** Critical Thinking

Enter your score for each activity. Add the scores together. Record your total score on the graph on page 115.

_____ Finding the Main Idea

_____ Recalling Facts

_____ Making Inferences

_____ Using Words

_____ Author's Approach

_____ Summarizing and Paraphrasing

_____ Critical Thinking

_____ **Total Score**

Personal Response

I wonder why _____

_____

_____

Self-Assessment

From reading this article, I have learned

_____

_____

What Happened to Glen and Bessie Hyde?

Glen and Bessie Hyde had just gotten married. Most couples would have planned to go off on a nice, quiet honeymoon. But that was not for Glen and Bessie. They wanted something more. They wanted an adventure. And they were willing to face danger to get it.

2   Glen and Bessie decided to raft some rivers. They would start on the Green River in Utah. Then they would move on to the Colorado River, with its wild torrents. Their trip would end hundreds of miles later in California. They knew the journey would be dangerous. But Glen, a farmer, loved river boating. And Bessie, an artist, was always ready to try new things.

3   Glen did have some experience. Two years earlier, he had made a boat trip through Idaho. On that trip, he had spent time with a boat expert. The man had shown Glen how to make a boat by hand. Now Glen had made his own boat. It was in this 20-foot wooden boat that he and Bessie would travel.

Shown here is a woman some people believe is Bessie Hyde. This picture was taken after Bessie Hyde disappeared on a rafting trip with her husband. Is she really Bessie Hyde? Nobody knows for sure.

4   The Hydes set out on October 20. They hoped to set three records. They wanted to make the fastest trip ever down the Colorado River. If they could do it, they would also be the first ones to go through every rapid. And Bessie would be the first woman ever to go down the Colorado River.

5   Things went well at first. Bessie made notes on all the things she saw. She noted each rapid. She wrote about the twists and turns in the river. She and Glen had their pictures taken by people they met. They made fast time. In early November, they entered the Grand Canyon. They made it safely through some bad rapids. On November 18, they stopped to eat dinner. They talked with a sightseer by the river. But after that, no one saw them again.

6   A month later, on December 19, their boat was found. It was floating in calm water at the bottom of the Grand Canyon. One of its ropes had caught on a rock. The boat was in perfect shape, and nothing was missing. People found Glen's and Bessie's clothes and hiking boots in the boat, along with a book with maps of the river. Glen's gun was still there. So were the notes Bessie had been keeping. There was plenty of food on board too. In short, everything was there except Glen and Bessie themselves.

7   People were completely puzzled. They looked for the Hydes for months. They searched the Grand Canyon and the Colorado River, but they found nothing.

8   What happened to Glen and Bessie? No one knows. But some ideas have been put forward. One is that Bessie killed Glen and then ran away to start a new life. This story spread in 1971. It began when a river guide told sightseers the story of the missing couple. One of the sightseers—an old woman—began to laugh. "I know what happened," she said. "I'm Bessie Hyde." The old woman went on to say that Glen had treated her badly. "He was beating me," the old woman said. "I stabbed him, threw him in the river, and hiked out."

9   Was this old woman really Bessie Hyde? And had she really killed Glen? The police didn't think so. They never charged her. Many people think the woman made the whole story up, but others are not so sure. They point out that the old woman was about as tall as Bessie. Her face looked like Bessie's too. These people wonder if perhaps the old woman was telling the truth.

10   In 1992 the story of Glen and Bessie took another turn. In that year, a woman named Georgie White died. For years, this woman had lived and boated along the Grand Canyon. But when she died, people learned she wasn't who she'd said she was. Her name wasn't Georgie. It was Bessie. Hidden in one of her dresser drawers was a gun—the same kind of gun the Hydes had carried. Also in the drawer lay a wedding certificate. It was made out to Glen and Bessie Hyde.

11   Was this woman Bessie Hyde? Some people think so. But others do not agree. They point out that river boating was Glen's love, not Bessie's. Why would she have spent her life doing it?

12   There are other ideas too. Maybe both Glen and Bessie lived through their boat ride. Maybe they wanted a new start in life, so they faked a boating accident. They could have hiked out of the canyon and begun new lives with new names someplace else. Or maybe they both drowned. The rapids they had to pass through were very rough. They might both have been washed over the side of the boat. But in that case, why weren't their bodies ever found?

13   The secret of Glen and Bessie lies in the Grand Canyon. But it is not likely that anyone will find it now. The Hydes had been hoping to set records and win fame. They didn't set any records. But they did become famous as the honeymoon couple who never returned. 🎗

A | Finding the Main Idea

One statement below tells the main idea of the article. One statement is too general, or too broad. The other statement explains only part of the article; it is too narrow. Label the statements using the following key:

M—Main Idea   B—Too Broad   N—Too Narrow

_____ 1. Glen and Bessie Hyde, just married, were on a rafting trip in the Grand Canyon when they disappeared. No one knows what happened to them.

_____ 2. Rafting in the Grand Canyon can be very dangerous, and more than one person have disappeared after rafting there.

_____ 3. Glen and Bessie Hyde got married in 1928. On October 20 of that year, they set out on a rafting trip. Someone saw and talked with them in the Grand Canyon on November 19.

Score 4 points for each correct answer.

_____ **Total Score:** Finding the Main Idea

B | Recalling Facts

How well do you remember the facts in the article? Put an X in the box next to the correct answer.

1. Glen and Bessie Hyde planned to end their rafting trip in

☐ a. the Grand Canyon.
☐ b. California.
☐ c. Colorado.

2. The last person to talk to Glen and Bessie Hyde was

☐ a. a sightseer.
☐ b. a park worker.
☐ c. one of their friends.

3. In 1971 a woman who said she was Bessie Hyde told sightseers that

☐ a. Glen had drowned on the trip down the Colorado River.
☐ b. she and Glen had fallen into the river, and only she had been able to swim to safety.
☐ c. she had stabbed Glen and thrown him in the river.

4. Some people thought that Georgie White was really Bessie Hyde because

☐ a. her art looked like the art that Bessie used to make.
☐ b. she kept a wedding certificate made out to Glen and Bessie Hyde in her dresser drawer.
☐ c. she told them that she had been married to Glen.

Score 4 points for each correct answer.

_____ **Total Score:** Recalling Facts

59

C Making Inferences

When you draw a conclusion that is not directly stated in the text, you are making an inference. Put an X in the box next to the statement that is a correct inference.

1.

☐ a. Glen and Bessie Hyde were willing to talk to strangers.

☐ b. The boat that Glen made was not strong enough to make it through rapids.

☐ c. Glen and Bessie Hyde always liked do what everyone else did.

2.

☐ a. Glen and Bessie always stayed near other people who were rafting down rivers too.

☐ b. Glen and Bessie had planned their river trip carefully.

☐ c. Most people thought that Glen and Bessie had been robbed before they disappeared.

Score 4 points for each correct answer.

_____ **Total Score:** Making Inferences

D Using Words

Put an X in the box next to the definition below that is closest in meaning to the underlined word.

1. You can tell that the young man and woman are on their honeymoon because they seem so much in love.

☐ a. a trip taken by a couple after their wedding

☐ b. the home of a group of honeybees

☐ c. a present given to a person who is leaving a job

2. When you raft down a river, you are almost sure to get wet.

☐ a. fly in an airplane

☐ b. float in a flat boat

☐ c. drive a truck or van

3. The boater shouted, "Get ready for anything! If these torrents flip our boat over, we could both drown!"

☐ a. a part of a river where the water is calm and slow

☐ b. a boat that can move through a body of water very quickly

☐ c. a part of a river where the water runs fast

4. The book is written for any sightseers who have come here to see castles along this river.

☐ a. people who can see into the future

☐ b. people who travel to see interesting sights

☐ c. artists who create beautiful objects

5. By accident, I <u>stabbed</u> myself with a knife while I was slicing carrots.

☐ a. ate or drank a food that is poison
☐ b. spent too much money
☐ c. pierced with a sharp, pointed object

6. When I read my birth <u>certificate</u>, I found out that I was born at 2:43 P.M.

☐ a. a paper that states that a given fact is true
☐ b. a person who knows that a given fact is true
☐ c. a fact that is known to be true

Score 4 points for each correct answer.

_____ **Total Score:** Using Words

E │ Author's Approach

Put an X in the box next to the correct answer.

1. The author uses the first sentence of the article to

☐ a. tell the reader that Glen and Bessie Hyde had not been married long.
☐ b. tell the reader that Glen and Bessie Hyde wanted adventure.
☐ c. compare Glen Hyde and Bessie Hyde.

2. What is the author's purpose in writing this article?

☐ a. to get the reader to raft down a river
☐ b. to tell the reader about a strange mystery
☐ c. to make readers afraid to go to the Grand Canyon

3. Choose the statement below that is the weakest argument for rafting down the Colorado River.

☐ a. Rafting can be exciting and fun.
☐ b. A rafting accident could kill you.
☐ c. When you raft, you see beautiful things up close.

Score 4 points for each correct answer.

_____ **Total Score:** Author's Approach

F Summarizing and Paraphrasing

Put an X in the box next to the correct answer.

1. Which summary says all the important things about the article?

- [ ] a. A woman who said she was the missing rafter Bessie Hyde came forward in 1971. She said she had killed her husband, Glen, in 1928. Even though she said she killed Glen, she was never charged with murder.

- [ ] b. Glen and Bessie Hyde disappeared while rafting down the Colorado River in 1928. Their boat was found in perfect shape, but they were gone. Maybe Bessie lived or maybe both Bessie and Glen died, but no one knows for sure.

- [ ] c. Glen and Bessie Hyde were people who didn't mind a little danger. That is why they decided to go rafting on wild rivers on their honeymoon in 1928. Glen built his own boat. Bessie took notes as they went down the rivers. They met many people along the way.

2. Which is the best paraphrase for the following sentence? "But some ideas have been put forward."

- [ ] a. But people have suggested a few ideas.
- [ ] b. But a few of the ideas are better than others.
- [ ] c. Some of the ideas, however, don't make any sense.

Score 4 points for each correct answer.

_____ **Total Score:** Summarizing and Paraphrasing

G Critical Thinking

Put an X in the box next to the correct answer.

1. Choose the statement below that states a fact.

- [ ] a. The story of what happened to Glen and Bessie is the most interesting mystery of the West.
- [ ] b. Glen and Bessie Hyde were foolish to start such a hard trip without more experience.
- [ ] c. Glen and Bessie Hyde were married in 1928.

2. Glen and Bessie Hyde were alike because

- [ ] a. both liked adventures.
- [ ] b. both were farmers.
- [ ] c. both were artists.

3. In 1971 a woman who said she was Bessie said she killed Glen. What did she say was the cause of her decision to kill him?

- [ ] a. She wanted all his money.
- [ ] b. She didn't really want to kill him. She killed him by accident.
- [ ] c. She was angry at Glen for treating her badly.

4. In which paragraph did you find the information or details to answer question 3?

- [ ] a. paragraph 8
- [ ] b. paragraph 9
- [ ] c. paragraph 12

5. Which lesson about life does this story teach?

☐ a. There is no reason to be afraid of taking a chance.

☐ b. Some things in life may always be mysteries.

☐ c. If you plan carefully, everything always works out right.

Score 4 points for each correct answer.

_____ **Total Score:** Critical Thinking

Enter your score for each activity. Add the scores together. Record your total score on the graph on page 115.

_____ Finding the Main Idea

_____ Recalling Facts

_____ Making Inferences

_____ Using Words

_____ Author's Approach

_____ Summarizing and Paraphrasing

_____ Critical Thinking

_____ **Total Score**

Personal Response

If you could ask the author of the article one question, what would it be? _____

_____

_____

Self-Assessment

While reading the article, _____

_____

was the easiest for me.

The Wreck of the Edmund Fitzgerald

EDMUND FITZGERALD
NO.2
500 CU.FT.   50 PERSONS

Some people say the ship never stood a chance. They say the S.S. *Edmund Fitzgerald* was cursed from the beginning. And, indeed, it did not get off to a very good start. When the ship was first put in the water in 1958, it sent a huge wave washing over the crowd. One man was so frightened that he had a heart attack and died.

2 Still, most people thought the *Edmund Fitzgerald* was a great ship. At 729 feet, it was as long as two city blocks. For years it was the biggest ship on the Great Lakes. It carried iron ore across Lake Superior. But on November 10, 1975, the *Edmund Fitzgerald* sank. All 29 men on board went down with it.

3 The *"Fitz"* took off from Superior, Wisconsin, on November 9. It was bound for Detroit. There it would drop off a huge load of ore. Captain Ernest McSorley knew that November trips across Lake Superior could be tricky. The weather could be bad. But he wasn't worried. McSorley had 44 years of experience. He knew

Shown here is the front of a lifeboat from the sunken ship Edmund Fitzgerald. *It is on display in Sault Ste. Marie, Michigan.*

how to handle storms. Besides, when the ship took off, the weather was quite serene.

4 By evening, things had changed. The wind had kicked up. A big storm was moving in. Captain McSorley radioed a nearby ship, the *Arthur M. Anderson*. McSorley talked with Bernie Cooper, the *Anderson's* captain. Both men agreed they should change their course. They headed farther to the north, toward Whitefish Bay. Going this way, they thought they would miss the worst part of the storm.

5 But the path of the storm changed. The two ships ended up right in the middle of it. The next morning, the wind was up to 48 miles per hour. Fifteen-foot waves slammed against the *Fitz* and the *Anderson*. As the day wore on, the storm got even worse. At 3:30 that afternoon, McSorley radioed Cooper again. He said the *Fitz* had begun to lean to one side. That meant water was seeping into the ship somehow. McSorley had turned on two pumps to get the water out. Still, he didn't want to take any chances. The *Anderson* was just a few miles away. "Will you stay by me 'til I get to Whitefish?" McSorley asked.

6 Captain Cooper was happy to say yes. "Charlie on that, *Fitzgerald,*" he said.

7 For the next four hours, the two ships struggled through the storm. By 7 P.M. the wind was blowing at 90 miles per hour, and the waves were 30 feet high. Still, McSorley felt he had things under control. At 7:10 P.M. Cooper asked him how he was doing. "We are holding our own," McSorley reported.

8 Those were the last words ever heard from the *Edmund Fitzgerald.*

9 The *Fitz* and the *Anderson* were 10 miles apart. Cooper was watching the *Fitz* on his radar. Radar sends out radio waves that bounce off objects. It is used to check where things that can't be seen are and how fast they are going. The *Fitzgerald* looked fine. At 7:15, however, the *Fitz* suddenly disappeared from the radar screen. Cooper couldn't believe it. What had happened? Only five minutes had passed since he had talked to McSorley. Yet now the ship was gone. Cooper called the Coast Guard to tell them the *Fitz* was missing. But it was too late. The *Fitzgerald,* with all its crew on board, had already sunk.

10 A few days later, the wrecked ship was found at the bottom of the lake. It lay in two pieces. The rest of the ship was completely gone. Clearly the ship had gone down fast. There had been no time to call for help and no time to use the lifeboats.

11 Over the years, people have tried to figure out exactly what happened that night. Some say the *Fitzgerald* hit a rock. The ship had passed through a shallow stretch of water earlier in the day. Many big rocks lay along this stretch. Did the *Fitz* hit one of them? Soon after passing this stretch, McSorley reported that his ship was taking on water. So perhaps the *Fitz* had been cut by a rock. If that let in enough water, the ship would have sunk. No cuts were found on the bottom of the wrecked ship. But a 200-foot piece in the middle of the *Fitz* was broken to bits. Perhaps that was where the cut came.

12 Other people think waves caused the *Fitzgerald* to sink. On Lake Superior, huge waves sometimes come in groups of three. These waves are called the Three Sisters. They are so strong and so close together that ships can't handle them. A direct hit by the Three Sisters can knock a ship right over. Just minutes before the *Fitzgerald* sank, two giant waves did hit the *Anderson.* Did a third wave suddenly form? If so, did these Three Sisters hit the *Fitzgerald?*

13 Some people think the problem lay in the ship itself. The *Fitzgerald* had lots of hatches. These doors could be opened to get iron ore in and out. All the hatches should have been locked during the journey. But perhaps they weren't. Perhaps a few never got locked. Or maybe some of the locks were broken. It is hard to believe the crew would have left hatches open during a storm. But the hatches on the wreck do look funny. They do look like they were never closed.

14 We may never know for sure why the *Edmund Fitzgerald* sank. All we know is that it went under quickly. It dropped like a rock. And it took 29 men with it. 🎗

A | Finding the Main Idea

One statement below tells the main idea of the article. One statement is too general, or too broad. The other statement explains only part of the article; it is too narrow. Label the statements using the following key:

M—Main Idea   B—Too Broad   N—Too Narrow

_____ 1. Whenever a storm hits on Lake Superior, even big ships can be hurt. In a bad storm, only skill and good luck can save a ship and its crew.

_____ 2. The S.S. *Edmund Fitzgerald* and the S.S. *Arthur M. Anderson* were both caught in a storm on Lake Superior. During the storm, winds blew at 90 miles per hour and the waves were 30 feet high.

_____ 3. An ore ship called the S.S. *Edmund Fitzgerald* sank in a storm on Lake Superior just after the captain reported everything was under control. Why it sank is a mystery.

Score 4 points for each correct answer.

_____ **Total Score:** Finding the Main Idea

B | Recalling Facts

How well do you remember the facts in the article? Put an X in the box next to the answer that correctly completes each statement.

1. The S.S. *Edmund Fitzgerald* began its last journey in
   □ a. November.
   □ b. August.
   □ c. September.

2. The captains of the *Edmund Fitzgerald* and the *Arthur M. Anderson* changed course so that they could
   □ a. reach Detroit sooner than planned.
   □ b. miss the worst part of the coming storm.
   □ c. get a better look at the coming storm.

3. When the *Edmund Fitzgerald* was found at the bottom of the lake, it was
   □ a. in perfect shape.
   □ b. upside down.
   □ c. cut in two.

4. The Three Sisters are
   □ a. women who help sailors on the Great Lakes.
   □ b. strong waves that come in groups of three.
   □ c. ghost boats that travel together.

Score 4 points for each correct answer.

_____ **Total Score:** Recalling Facts

C Making Inferences

When you draw a conclusion that is not directly stated in the text, you are making an inference. Put an X in the box next to the statement that is a correct inference.

1.

☐ a. Even a big ship can sink in a few minutes if it is hurt badly enough.

☐ b. Even ships that have sunk can be seen on a radar screen.

☐ c. If Captain Cooper had called the Coast Guard earlier, the *Fitzgerald* would probably not have sunk.

2.

☐ a. No one ever heard of the *Edmund Fitzgerald* until it sank.

☐ b. The Coast Guard never goes out onto Lake Superior during a storm.

☐ c. It was not possible for people on the deck of the *Anderson* to see the *Fitzgerald* as it sank.

Score 4 points for each correct answer.

_____ **Total Score:** Making Inferences

D Using Words

Put an X in the box next to the definition below that is closest in meaning to the underlined word.

1. Our old car seemed underlined cursed because every time we took it on a trip, something bad happened to it.

☐ a. very fast
☐ b. not lucky
☐ c. real

2. Miners took the ore they dug up to a mill to get the gold separated from it.

☐ a. another name for paper money
☐ b. a type of tree that turns color in the fall
☐ c. rock from which metal can be taken

3. The peaceful cat looked serene.

☐ a. nervous
☐ b. angry
☐ c. calm

4. We found water seeping into the house through a crack in the floor.

☐ a. entering slowly
☐ b. attacking fiercely
☐ c. touching lightly

5. The only part of the <u>wrecked</u> car that still worked was the radio.

☐ a. brand new

☐ b. ruined

☐ c. perfect

6. The crew climbed into the <u>lifeboats</u> and got away just before the ship sank.

☐ a. small, strong boats

☐ b. huge ships

☐ c. boats where parties are held

> Score 4 points for each correct answer.
>
> _____ **Total Score:** Using Words

E | Author's Approach

Put an X in the box next to the correct answer.

1. The author uses the first sentence of the article to

☐ a. suggest to the reader that something bad was going to happen to the S.S. *Edmund Fitzgerald.*

☐ b. describe the way the S.S. *Edmund Fitzgerald* looked right after it was made.

☐ c. compare the S.S. *Edmund Fitzgerald* and the S.S. *Arthur M. Anderson.*

2. Choose the statement below that best describes the author's opinion in paragraph 3.

☐ a. It was so important to get the ore to Detroit that the captain didn't mind facing danger.

☐ b. Captain McSorley should have known the weather would change later that day.

☐ c. It made sense for the captain to think the *Edmund Fitzgerald* would be safe on the trip.

3. The author probably wrote this article in order to

☐ a. show that the *Edmund Fitzgerald* was not made well enough.

☐ b. tell an interesting story about a ship in trouble.

☐ c. get ships to stay off Lake Superior in November.

> Score 4 points for each correct answer.
>
> _____ **Total Score:** Author's Approach

F Summarizing and Paraphrasing

Put an X in the box next to the correct answer.

1. Which summary says all the important things about the article?

☐ a. The S.S. *Edmund Fitzgerald* sank in a storm on Lake Superior in 1975, killing 29 crew members. Minutes before the ship sank, its captain said everything was under control. People have different ideas about why it sank, but no one knows for sure.

☐ b. The captains of the S.S. *Edmund Fitzgerald* and the S.S. *Arthur M. Anderson* decided to change their courses when a big storm was on the way. They stayed in touch for hours as they struggled with the storm.

☐ c. The S.S. *Edmund Fitzgerald* might have run into sharp rocks; it might have been hit by the Three Sisters; or it might have had water come in through its open hatches.

2. Which sentence means the same thing as the following sentence? "The *Fitz* was bound for Detroit."

☐ a. The *Fitz* was going away from Detroit.
☐ b. The *Fitz* had been repaired in Detroit.
☐ c. The *Fitz* was going to Detroit.

Score 4 points for each correct answer.

_____ **Total Score:** Summarizing and Paraphrasing

G Critical Thinking

Put an X in the box next to the correct answer.

1. Choose the statement below that states an opinion.

☐ a. The S.S. *Edmund Fitzgerald* disappeared from the *Anderson's* radar screen at 7:15 P.M. on November 10, 1975.

☐ b. For years, the S.S. *Edmund Fitzgerald*, at 729 feet long, was the biggest ship on the Great Lakes.

☐ c. Being the captain of a ship on the Great Lakes is one of the hardest jobs in the world.

2. From information in the article, you can predict that

☐ a. ship captains will be very careful during Lake Superior storms.

☐ b. no one will ever set out on a journey across Lake Superior in November ever again.

☐ c. ship captains on Lake Superior will stop using radar to see where things are on the lake.

3. The S.S. *Edmund Fitzgerald* and the S.S. *Arthur M. Anderson* are alike because

☐ a. both arrived at home safely after a terrible storm.
☐ b. both were on Lake Superior during a terrible storm.
☐ c. both sank in a November storm.

4. What could be the effect of leaving the hatches open on an ore ship during a storm?

☐ a. Water could get into the ship, perhaps sinking it.
☐ b. People could not load the iron ore into the ship.
☐ c. The ship could not use its radar.

5. Which lesson about life does this story teach?

☐ a. Sailing is a restful and pleasant way to travel.

☐ b. You can never be too careful.

☐ c. People usually forget about a sad event right after it happens.

Score 4 points for each correct answer.

_____ **Total Score:** Critical Thinking

Enter your score for each activity. Add the scores together. Record your total score on the graph on page 115.

_____ Finding the Main Idea

_____ Recalling Facts

_____ Making Inferences

_____ Using Words

_____ Author's Approach

_____ Summarizing and Paraphrasing

_____ Critical Thinking

_____ **Total Score**

Personal Response

I can't believe _____

_____

Self-Assessment

One good question about this article that was not asked would be _____

_____

Killer Flu

People wanted a break. They had seen enough death. World War I had left millions dead. But there was to be no relief. In 1918, a few months before the war ended, a new killer showed up. It was influenza—or, simply, the "flu." In less than a year, this virus would kill more than 20 million people. That's more than any other flu has ever killed. Even today, experts wonder what made this flu so deadly.

2   There are all kinds of flu. Any of them can kill. Usually, flu kills the very old or the very young. That makes sense. Their bodies are the weakest. But this flu was different. It killed strong young adults. Of course, the flu was so deadly that it killed people of all ages. But it was especially hard on those aged 15 to 34. Their death rate was higher than that of any other age group. To this day, no one knows why.

3   This much was known about the flu. It entered the body through the nose or mouth. People breathed it in.

Influenza killed more than 20 million people around the world in 1918. This picture shows nurses caring for the sick in outdoor tents in Lawrence, Massachusetts.

Once it was in, it attacked the whole body. Victims developed high fevers and chills. Their heads and their muscles throbbed. Their stomachs hurt, and their throats got sore. They coughed. They had trouble breathing. Most people got better. But one out of every 20 people who caught the flu died from it. And one out of every five people in the world caught it. Some experts think the numbers are even higher. They say more than half the people in the world got the flu.

4   The flu burst onto the scene in the spring of 1918. People didn't think much about it at first. They thought the victims simply had caught a cold. All the sick people had to do, they thought, was rest and drink lots of water. But these people did not have a cold. They had a deadly sickness that no one had ever seen before. Suddenly people were dying left and right.

5   The flu struck everywhere. It swept through cities. It wiped out villages. It hit hot, dry towns in Africa and cold, snowy towns in Canada. It swept through the hills of China. It hit the jungles of Brazil. It struck the rich and the poor. President Woodrow Wilson caught the flu. Future president Franklin Roosevelt did too. Both men lived. But for a time they were quite sick.

6   It took the flu just a few days to kill a victim. Sometimes it took just a few hours. In one case, four women sat down to play an evening game of cards.

They felt fine when they started playing. But their game didn't last long. By the next morning, three of the women had gotten sick and died. In other cases, people got sick walking to work and died on the job later the same day.

7   In some places, bodies were piled up in the streets. People couldn't bury the dead fast enough. They couldn't make coffins fast enough. Things were not much better for the victims who lived. There were not enough doctors and nurses. Hospitals had no empty beds.

8   No one knew whom or what to blame. Some people said this flu came from Spain. In fact, at the time it was called the "Spanish flu." But experts later decided it didn't start there. So where did it come from? People came up with some pretty wild ideas. A few Americans blamed the Germans. They were the enemy in World War I. Did they somehow spread the flu? Both sides had used poison gas during the war. Had all that deadly gas created the flu? Other people blamed such things as coal dust, bad air, and dirty dishwater. In fact, experts think that none of these were to blame. The truth is that even today no one knows how the flu started. Today's scientists think that the flu comes from birds. But no one knows how the 1918 flu jumped to humans. And no one knows why it was so deadly.

9   People tried everything to avoid this flu. They wore masks over their mouths. They stayed away from crowds. To enter some towns, people needed a signed note from a doctor. Stores could not have sales because that would bring out too many people. And if someone died, the church service could last only 15 minutes.

10   When World War I ended, Americans celebrated. They held parties and parades. These events helped to spread the flu. Also, many soldiers brought the flu home with them. So no matter how hard people tried to avoid it, the flu was all around them.

11   And then, as quickly as it came, the flu went away. No one knows why, but by 1919 the worst was over. The flu died out completely. Only the questions lingered. How did this flu take hold in humans? What made it so deadly? And what made it disappear? Experts still have no final answers. But there is another question. Will it return? Professor John Oxford has studied the problem. "No one expects the 1918 flu to come back again," he said. That's the good news. But Oxford went on to warn that a new type of flu might appear the same way this one did. There's no telling what could happen then.

A Finding the Main Idea

One statement below tells the main idea of the article. One statement is too general, or too broad. The other statement explains only part of the article; it is too narrow. Label the statements using the following key:

M—Main Idea   B—Too Broad   N—Too Narrow

_____ 1. The flu of 1918 did not kill everyone who caught it. Only about one in 20 people who came down with the flu died of it.

_____ 2. In 1918 a deadly flu swept over the whole world, killing millions. No one knows where it came from, how it began to attack humans, or why it finally stopped.

_____ 3. You may not think that the flu is dangerous, but if you knew about the flu of 1918, you might change your mind.

Score 4 points for each correct answer.

_____ **Total Score**: Finding the Main Idea

B Recalling Facts

How well do you remember the facts in the article? Put an X in the box next to the answer that correctly completes each statement.

1. The 1918 flu was most deadly for
   - ☐ a. babies and small children.
   - ☐ b. young adults between 15 and 34.
   - ☐ c. adults above 65 years old.

2. People became sick when they
   - ☐ a. were bitten by an animal that had the flu.
   - ☐ b. ate food that held the flu.
   - ☐ c. breathed in the flu.

3. Today, scientists think that the flu comes from
   - ☐ a. birds.
   - ☐ b. Spain.
   - ☐ c. dirty water.

4. The flu died out in
   - ☐ a. 1918.
   - ☐ b. 1919.
   - ☐ c. 1920.

Score 4 points for each correct answer.

_____ **Total Score**: Recalling Facts

C | Making Inferences

When you draw a conclusion that is not directly stated in the text, you are making an inference. Put an X in the box next to the statement that is a correct inference.

1.

- [ ] a. If one person in a family died from the flu, all the other family members knew they would die from it too.
- [ ] b. If you stayed away from other people, you were less likely to catch the flu.
- [ ] c. Because hospitals were kept clean, they were the best places to go to escape the flu.

2.

- [ ] a. The flu was strongest in places that were not very hot and not very cold.
- [ ] b. If the soldiers had not come home after the war, no one in America would have gotten the flu.
- [ ] c. If you caught even a little cold in 1918, people were probably afraid to be near you.

Score 4 points for each correct answer.

_____ **Total Score:** Making Inferences

D | Using Words

Put an X in the box next to the definition below that is closest in meaning to the underlined word.

1. Women in their 20s give birth at a higher rate than women in their 30s.

- [ ] a. a measure that compares one thing to another
- [ ] b. an especially important day of the year
- [ ] c. news of events that happened during the day

2. After she ate the whole pizza, her stomach throbbed, so she went to bed.

- [ ] a. felt better
- [ ] b. got smaller
- [ ] c. hurt

3. After the king and queen died, their bodies were laid in golden coffins.

- [ ] a. books about people who died
- [ ] b. boxes in which people are buried
- [ ] c. times set aside to remember people who died

4. When I walk my puppy, I avoid the house where the meanest dog in the neighborhood lives.

- [ ] a. keep away from
- [ ] b. go as close as possible to
- [ ] c. wait for

5. The team <u>rejoiced</u> when they won the big game.

   ☐ a. paid attention to someone in charge
   ☐ b. got together to do a job
   ☐ c. marked an event by having a good time

6. After the cookies were gone, only a few crumbs <u>lingered</u> at the bottom of the bag.

   ☐ a. tasted good
   ☐ b. went away
   ☐ c. were left

Score 4 points for each correct answer.

_____ **Total Score:** Using Words

E Author's Approach

Put an X in the box next to the correct answer.

1. The main purpose of the first paragraph is to

   ☐ a. tell what the article will be about.
   ☐ b. tell where the flu came from.
   ☐ c. tell when World War I ended.

2. What is the author's purpose in writing this article?

   ☐ a. to make people worried about getting sick
   ☐ b. to get people to go to their doctor if they have a cold
   ☐ c. to tell about a time when the flu was a great danger

3. From the statements below, choose the one that you believe the author would agree with.

   ☐ a. If people had been more careful, they could have avoided getting the flu.
   ☐ b. The 1918 flu was a terrible event.
   ☐ c. Doctors should have been able to stop the flu from spreading.

Score 4 points for each correct answer.

_____ **Total Score:** Author's Approach

F | Summarizing and Paraphrasing

Put an X in the box next to the correct answer.

1. Which summary says all the important things about the article?

☐ a. When people caught the flu of 1918, they developed high fevers and got headaches, sore throats, and stomachaches. They coughed and had trouble breathing. Many of the victims died quickly.

☐ b. No one knows how the flu of 1918 began or how it ended. It spread all over the world at the end of World War I, killing about 20 million people. No one knows whether a flu like it will ever come again.

☐ c. In 1918 soldiers were coming home from fighting World War I. Some of them carried the flu with them. When they got back home, they gave the flu to their friends and families.

2. Which sentence means the same thing as the following sentence? "Suddenly people were dying left and right."

☐ a. Without warning, the dying people left.

☐ b. Some people who were left started to die.

☐ c. All at once, people all around were dying.

Score 4 points for each correct answer.

_____ **Total Score:** Summarizing and Paraphrasing

G | Critical Thinking

Put an X in the box next to the correct answer.

1. Choose the statement below that states a fact.

☐ a. The 1918 flu was the worst thing that has ever happened in the world.

☐ b. Trying to avoid the 1918 flu, many people wore masks over their mouths.

☐ c. Doctors will probably be able to stop any other virus from killing people in the future.

2. From information in the article, you can predict that

☐ a. the world will never see a flu like the 1918 flu.

☐ b. the world could experience a flu like the 1918 flu.

☐ c. doctors will be able to save everyone who gets the flu if it comes again.

3. The flu and a cold are alike because

☐ a. both can kill people in just a few hours.

☐ b. both are spread to humans by birds.

☐ c. both may cause a person to cough.

4. What was the cause of the decision by some towns to let in only people who had a doctor's note?

☐ a. The towns wanted to keep out people who had the flu.

☐ b. The towns wanted to keep out poor people who didn't have enough money for a doctor.

☐ c. The towns wanted to find out the names of good doctors.

5. How is the killer flu of 1918 an example of something that is still unsolved?

☐ a. Millions of people died of the flu.

☐ b. No one knows how the flu began or why it ended.

☐ c. No one knows how the flu is spread between people.

Score 4 points for each correct answer.

_____ **Total Score:** Critical Thinking

Enter your score for each activity. Add the scores together. Record your total score on the graph on page 115.

_____ Finding the Main Idea

_____ Recalling Facts

_____ Making Inferences

_____ Using Words

_____ Author's Approach

_____ Summarizing and Paraphrasing

_____ Critical Thinking

_____ **Total Score**

Personal Response

What was most surprising or interesting to you about this article? _____

_____

_____

Self-Assessment

One of the things I did best when reading this article was

_____

I believe I did this well because _____

_____

Compare and Contrast

Pick two articles in Unit Two that tell about something strange that happened to a whole group of people.
Use information from the articles to fill in this chart.

Title	To what group of people did a strange thing happen?	When and where did the strange event take place?	What is still unsolved about the mystery?

Which of these strange events is more mysterious? Which way of explaining the mystery makes the most sense to you? Tell why.

_____

_____

UNIT THREE

The Murder of Emmett Till

Mamie Till Mobley had once lived in the South. So she knew what life was like for African Americans there. She knew how hard it was. In 1955 there were many things African Americans were not allowed to do. They couldn't swim at "white" beaches. They couldn't drink from "white" water fountains. They couldn't sit at the front of the bus. The list went on and on.

2   Mobley's 14-year-old son, Emmett Till, had grown up in the North. He didn't know how things worked in the South. In 1955 he was invited to visit relatives in Mississippi. The relatives promised Mobley that Emmett would be safe. Mobley had her doubts, but in the end she let him go.

3   Before Emmett left, Mobley tried to explain to him how much racism he would see. She told him that white people might dislike him just because he was African American. She told him to be careful. "Don't start up any conversations with white people," she warned him.

This picture shows people outside the Tallahatchie courthouse just before the beginning of the trial of J. W. Milam and Roy Bryant for the killing of a 14-year-old African American boy.

More than anything, she wanted Emmett to return safely. "If you have to humble yourself, then just do it. Get on your knees if you have to," she told him.

4   On August 21 Emmett arrived in Mississippi. He stayed at the home of his great uncle, Moses Wright. On August 24 Emmett walked into a grocery store with some other young people. They had all been picking cotton under a hot sun and wanted to cool off. Roy and Carolyn Bryant, a white couple, were the owners of the store.

5   Later, some of the young people said that Emmett whistled at Carolyn. It is not clear why he would have done that. What is known is that his mother had taught him to whistle as a way to get over a serious speech difficulty. As a child, Emmett had stuttered. It helped him if he whistled before he said a hard word. In any event, Carolyn Bryant thought Emmett was whistling *at* her.

6   Three nights later, on August 28, Roy Bryant and his half brother, J. W. Milam, went to the home of Emmett's great uncle. They carried guns with them. Bryant and Milam dragged Emmett from his bed and took him away. After they beat him up, they shot him in the head, tied a large metal fan around his neck, and then dumped his body in a river.

7   Three days later, the police fished Emmett Till's body out of the river. Officials were humiliated by how badly the boy had been beaten. So they sent his body home in a sealed coffin. They told Mamie Till Mobley not to open it. But Mobley didn't listen to them. She opened the coffin—and was horrified by what she saw. She decided to let photographers take pictures of her son's body. "Let the world see what I've seen," she said. Photos of Emmett's beaten face shocked the world.

8   Back in Mississippi, the police picked up Roy Bryant and J. W. Milam. The police charged them with murder. In court, Moses Wright pointed them out. He said they were the men who took Emmett from his home in the middle of the night.

9   There was no doubt that Bryant and Milam were the killers. But that didn't matter. The jury was made up of 12 white men. There were no African Americans on it. In 1955 there was no way an all-white jury would take the side of an African American. They would not go against two white men in this kind of case.

10   The jury took just 67 minutes to decide. One of the group said it could have been quicker, but they took time to drink sodas. Bill Minor, a reporter, said he heard the group laughing and joking.

11   The jury decided that Bryant and Milam did not kill Emmett. Later, the two men admitted they had killed Emmett. They told their story to a magazine for $4,000.

They knew they could tell the truth safely. Under the law, the police could not charge them twice for the same crime. So the murder of Emmett Till stayed officially unsolved.

12   But the story did not end there. The jury's decision angered people around the world. Mobley began her own fight to get the case opened again. She wanted justice for her son. She later wrote, "I would not harbor any hatred towards whites. But I would no longer accept their hatred of me or black people. I had learned what their hatred had cost me."

13   Mamie Till Mobley kept up her fight until she died in 2003. By then, Roy Bryant and J. W. Milam had also died. But the case did not go away. A man named Keith Beauchamp studied the murder for nine years. He made a movie called *The Untold Story of Emmett Louis Till.* Beauchamp discovered that Bryant and Milam may not have acted alone. Nine other people might have been involved. Five of them were still alive.

14   At last, in 2004, the U.S. Department of Justice opened the case again. Everyone knew that after 50 years it would not be easy to prove who saw what and when. So some parts of the murder would probably never be solved. Still, reopening the case sent a clear message. No longer could people get away with this kind of murder.

A | Finding the Main Idea

One statement below tells the main idea of the article. One statement is too general, or too broad. The other statement explains only part of the article; it is too narrow. Label the statements using the following key:

M—Main Idea   **B—Too Broad**   **N—Too Narrow**

_____ 1. The justice system of the United States has not always worked well, as the family of young Emmett Till discovered.

_____ 2. Emmett Till's mother warned him that he should be careful when he visited the South. For example, she told him not to start conversations with white people.

_____ 3. While visiting Mississippi, 14-year-old African American Emmett Till was killed by white people. His killers were not punished. The unsolved case has now been opened again.

Score 4 points for each correct answer.

_____ **Total Score:** Finding the Main Idea

B | Recalling Facts

How well do you remember the facts in the article? Put an X in the box next to the answer that correctly completes each statement.

1. Emmett Till got into trouble when he

☐ a. started a conversation with Carolyn Bryant.
☐ b. whistled while talking.
☐ c. started picking cotton in Mississippi.

2. After Roy Bryant and J. W. Milam beat up Emmett, they

☐ a. buried him in the woods.
☐ b. took him back to his great uncle's home.
☐ c. shot him and threw his body in a river.

3. After they were found innocent in court, Roy Bryant and J. W. Milam

☐ a. admitted that they killed Emmett.
☐ b. refused to say whether they killed Emmett.
☐ c. repeated many times that they had not killed Emmett.

4. The U.S. Department of Justice opened Emmett Till's case again in

☐ a. 1975.
☐ b. 2001.
☐ c. 2004.

Score 4 points for each correct answer.

_____ **Total Score:** Recalling Facts

C | Making Inferences

When you draw a conclusion that is not directly stated in the text, you are making an inference. Put an X in the box next to the statement that is a correct inference.

1.

☐ a. The jury took a short time to make their decision because they knew Bryant and Milam were innocent.

☐ b. At first, Moses Wright did not think that Bryant and Milam meant to hurt Emmett when they came to his house at night.

☐ c. Mamie Till Mobley thought that her son would be safer in the North than in the South.

2.

☐ a. Bryant and Milam were ashamed of themselves after they killed Emmett.

☐ b. Mamie Till Mobley did not always follow orders from officials.

☐ c. Most likely, Bryant and Milam thought the case would be reopened.

Score 4 points for each correct answer.

_____ **Total Score:** Making Inferences

D | Using Words

Put an X in the box next to the definition below that is closest in meaning to the underlined word.

1. Not letting African Americans drink from the same water fountain as white people was clear <u>racism</u>.

☐ a. a contest in which one person tries to run faster than another

☐ b. the act of identifying a person's race

☐ c. unfair treatment based on race

2. Because the boy <u>stuttered</u> badly, people listening to him kept finishing his words for him.

☐ a. repeated sounds without control

☐ b. said what was on one's mind without thinking about what the effect would be

☐ c. had trouble walking without help

3. The boy was <u>humiliated</u> when he had to wear old clothes to school.

☐ a. embarrassed

☐ b. proud

☐ c. happy

4. After the woman died, the police charged her husband with <u>murder</u>.

☐ a. the crime of hurting someone

☐ b. the crime of killing someone

☐ c. the crime of stealing something

5. People on a <u>jury</u> have to listen to the facts carefully before they decide who is to blame for a crime.

☐ a. a time set aside for having fun, away from everyday life

☐ b. a group of people who take turns answering questions from an audience

☐ c. a group of people who decide whether someone broke the law

6. <u>Hatred</u> of the enemy keeps soldiers fighting.

☐ a. love

☐ b. deep dislike

☐ c. friendship

Score 4 points for each correct answer.

_____ **Total Score:** Using Words

E | Author's Approach

Put an X in the box next to the correct answer.

1. The main purpose of the first paragraph is to

☐ a. show how hard things were for African Americans in the South.

☐ b. show that Mamie Till Mobley loved her son, Emmett.

☐ c. tell why Mamie Till Mobley's son, Emmett, wanted to visit the South.

2. Choose the statement below that best describes the author's opinion in paragraph 10.

☐ a. The jury was trying hard to be fair.

☐ b. The jury did not take its job seriously.

☐ c. Bill Minor, the reporter, was not fair to the jury.

3. The author tells this story mainly by

☐ a. telling about events in time order.

☐ b. comparing different people.

☐ c. using his or her imagination.

Score 4 points for each correct answer.

_____ **Total Score:** Author's Approach

F Summarizing and Paraphrasing

Put an X in the box next to the correct answer.

1. Which summary says all the important things about the article?

☐ a. In 1955 young Emmett Till wanted to visit his great uncle in Mississippi. His mother told him to be careful in the South. She knew that life was hard for African Americans there. She wanted him to stay safe.

☐ b. Roy Bryant and his half brother, J. W. Milam, killed Emmett Till, a 14-year-old African American, for whistling at a white woman. After they were found innocent, they admitted in a magazine story that they really had done the crime.

☐ c. Emmett Till, a 14-year-old African American from the North, was visiting in the South when he upset a white woman. Her husband and his half brother killed Emmett but were later found innocent of the crime. Emmett's mother wanted justice and fought to get the case opened again. It was reopened in 2004.

2. Which sentence means the same thing as the following sentence? "If you have to humble yourself, then just do it."

☐ a. If others make you lose your temper, just be careful.

☐ b. If you have to give up your pride, just give it up.

☐ c. If you have to fight for your rights, don't be afraid.

Score 4 points for each correct answer.

_____ **Total Score:** Summarizing and Paraphrasing

G Critical Thinking

Put an X in the box next to the correct answer.

1. Choose the statement below that states an opinion.

☐ a. The jury took 67 minutes to decide that Roy Bryant and J. W. Milam were innocent.

☐ b. Emmett Till's family should never give up looking for the truth about who killed him.

☐ c. Mamie Till Mobley grew up in the South.

2. From information in the article, you can predict that if police find out who helped to kill Emmett,

☐ a. they will take them to court.

☐ b. they will let them go.

☐ c. no one will care.

3. What was the effect of Emmett's whistle in Carolyn Bryant's store?

☐ a. Bryant thought Emmett was whistling at her.

☐ b. Bryant thought Emmett was being nice.

☐ c. Bryant thought Emmett was trying not to stutter.

4. In which paragraph did you find your information or details to answer question 3?

☐ a. paragraph 4

☐ b. paragraph 5

☐ c. paragraph 8

5. How is the murder of Emmett Till an example of something that is still unsolved?

☐ a. No one knows where Emmett Till was killed or what happened to his body.

☐ b. No one knows why anyone was angry enough to kill Emmett Till.

☐ c. No one knows whether everyone who helped to kill Emmett Till has been found.

Score 4 points for each correct answer.

_____ **Total Score:** Critical Thinking

Enter your score for each activity. Add the scores together. Record your total score on the graph on page 115.

_____ Finding the Main Idea

_____ Recalling Facts

_____ Making Inferences

_____ Using Words

_____ Author's Approach

_____ Summarizing and Paraphrasing

_____ Critical Thinking

_____ **Total Score**

Personal Response

I agree with the author because _____

_____

Self-Assessment

Before reading this article, I already knew _____

_____

Canada's Lake Monster

One evening in 2004, a woman looked out over Lake Okanagan. She saw birds taking off from the water's surface. Then she heard a strange thumping sound. Something in the water began to splash and spray. The woman saw three shiny humps rise and fall. Some sort of huge creature was swimming in the lake! Frightened, the woman ran back into her house to call for help. But then she stopped short. She didn't know what number to dial. After all, who would believe her?

2   What this woman saw—or thought she saw—was a lake monster. The most notorious lake monster in the world is the Loch Ness monster in Scotland. But Lake Okanagan in British Columbia, Canada, has one too. It is called Ogopogo. Like the Loch Ness monster, it has been seen hundreds of times. Some folks don't believe in its existence. But others are sure it is out there, hiding somewhere in this 80-mile-long lake.

3   The first people to see Ogopogo·were the native tribes of Canada. Hundreds of years ago they drew

This is a picture of Lake Okanagan in British Columbia. It is where the lake monster Ogopogo is supposed to live.

pictures of what looks like a lake monster. They even had a name for it. The Chinook called it the "wicked one" or the "great beast on the lake." The Salish called it N'ha-a-tik, or "lake demon." These native people feared the fiend. Whenever they crossed the lake, they took a small animal with them. They would toss it into the lake as a gift to the monster. They hoped the monster would be pleased and would leave them alone.

4   When Europeans settled near the lake, they also saw the monster. In 1880 one woman said, "I saw something that looked like a huge tree trunk or log floating on the lake." But she did not think it could be a tree or a log. She said, "It was going against the current and not with it."

5   In 1936 two boys named Geoff Tozer and Andy Aikman spent many hours on the lake. These boys had heard about Ogopogo. They didn't believe the stories. But they changed their minds when they went on a four-day camping and fishing trip.

6   On the first day, the boys caught a fish. They were so excited they didn't notice a large group of birds nearby. Their boat drifted closer to the birds. Then, without warning, the birds screeched loudly and flew straight up. A huge creature leaped out of the water and grabbed one of the birds in its mouth. Just a couple of seconds later, the creature disappeared again.

7 "Andy and I were scared to death," Geoff later recalled. "We spent the night as far up from the lake as possible." They cut their fishing trip short and went home the next day. Geoff said that the monster was about 14 feet long and as big around as a "telephone pole."

8 Like these boys, most people have gotten only a brief look at Ogopogo. It doesn't show up on any schedule. So people are often caught by surprise. By the time they realize what they're seeing, it's gone.

9 People have described the monster in many ways. Some have said it has a head like a horse or goat. Geoff Tozer said its head was "like a cow's." People have said the monster is green or gray or black or just a strange color. Its length has also been hard to determine. No one has ever seen its whole body at once. Some people have said it could be 50 feet long. Others say it is closer to 15 or 20 feet long.

10 But does Ogopogo really exist? Or is it just a product of people's imagination? In 1990, a Japanese camera crew came to find out. They brought all sorts of fancy equipment with them. Arlene Gaal, a writer of three books on Ogopogo, was their guide. One day, she said, she and the crew saw something "like a huge serpent moving slowly, turning in large circles."

11 Don Defty drove one of the cars for the crew. He, too, saw something. Defty was on high ground looking down at the lake. "You could see 30 to 40 feet away, under the water," he said. According to him, the monster "was large and looked like it had something like flippers." The crew hoped to capture Ogopogo's image with its cameras. But when the film came back, it only showed water being churned about. There was no clear picture of a lake monster. The crew kept looking, but they never got any good footage of Ogopogo.

12 That did not discourage Arlene Gaal. "I know something exists," she said. "There have been hundreds of sightings—too many to be explained away by any other cause."

13 In 2001 the town of Kelowna offered a reward of two million dollars to anyone who could take a good photo of the monster. So far no one has claimed the money. No one has taken that one nice, clear picture. Maybe no one ever will. But does that mean that Ogopogo doesn't exist? Or does it just mean that this lake monster is smarter—and perhaps a bit more shy—than people realize?

A | Finding the Main Idea

One statement below tells the main idea of the article. One statement is too general, or too broad. The other statement explains only part of the article; it is too narrow. Label the statements using the following key:

M—Main Idea   **B—Too Broad**   **N—Too Narrow**

_____ 1. Some people say that a huge monster lives in Lake Okanagan in British Columbia, but others are not sure that it exists.

_____ 2. Long ago, when native people would cross Lake Okanagan, they would throw in a small animal as a gift to the monster of the lake.

_____ 3. No matter which part of the world you may live in, there is probably a fascinating tale of a local monster.

Score 4 points for each correct answer.

_____ **Total Score:** Finding the Main Idea

B | Recalling Facts

How well do you remember the facts in the article? Put an X in the box next to the answer that correctly completes each statement.

1. Everyone who has seen Ogopogo agrees that it
   - ☐ a. is large.
   - ☐ b. looks like a cow.
   - ☐ c. has a head like a horse.

2. Geoff Tozer and Andy Aikman saw the creature eat
   - ☐ a. a small child.
   - ☐ b. some fish.
   - ☐ c. a bird.

3. A Japanese crew described the monster as a
   - ☐ a. demon.
   - ☐ b. huge serpent.
   - ☐ c. dragon.

4. In 2001 the town of Kelowna said that whoever takes a clear picture of Ogopogo would get a reward of
   - ☐ a. a trip to Lake Okanagan.
   - ☐ b. $1,000.
   - ☐ c. two million dollars.

Score 4 points for each correct answer.

_____ **Total Score:** Recalling Facts

C | Making Inferences

When you draw a conclusion that is not directly stated in the text, you are making an inference. Put an X in the box next to the statement that is a correct inference.

1.

☐ a. Everyone who has fished or swum in Lake Okanagan more than a few times has probably seen Ogopogo.

☐ b. People of the town of Kelowna don't think anyone will ever take a clear picture of Ogopogo.

☐ c. Geoff Tozer and Andy Aikman are hoping that they will see Ogopogo again someday.

2.

☐ a. It is hard to take a good picture of an animal that splashes a lot and swims fast.

☐ b. Lake Okanagan probably has no fish because Ogopogo eats them all.

☐ c. If you used a good camera, you would surely be able to get a good picture of Ogopogo.

Score 4 points for each correct answer.

_____ **Total Score:** Making Inferences

D | Using Words

Put an X in the box next to the definition below that is closest in meaning to the underlined word.

1. The man was <u>notorious</u> for coming to work late every day.

☐ a. not well known

☐ b. truthful

☐ c. generally known and talked about

2. My brother questions the <u>existence</u> of ghosts.

☐ a. being; something that is

☐ b. make-believe

☐ c. something that is old

3. The <u>fiend</u> ate people who came near it, so people were afraid of it.

☐ a. kind and gentle creature

☐ b. very bad or harmful creature

☐ c. funny and joking creature

4. The frightened child imagined that a <u>demon</u> was hiding under his bed.

☐ a. a friendly person or thing

☐ b. a scary place

☐ c. an evil spirit

5. The long <u>serpent</u> slid over the rocks and then silently disappeared into a hole in the ground.

☐ a. a snake

☐ b. a deer

☐ c. a dog

6. The reporter left the <u>footage</u> of the big fire in her car, so it wasn't shown on the evening television news report.

☐ a. a blue or purple color

☐ b. a piece of movie film

☐ c. good feelings

Score 4 points for each correct answer.

_____ **Total Score:** Using Words

E   Author's Approach

Put an X in the box next to the correct answer.

1. What is the author's purpose in writing this article?

☐ a. to get the reader to look for monsters that may be hiding near the reader's home

☐ b. to tell the reader about a strange beast that may or may not exist

☐ c. to describe Lake Okanagan and British Columbia

2. Choose the statement below that is the weakest argument for believing in Ogopogo.

☐ a. Hundreds of people claim that they have seen Ogopogo.

☐ b. There are drawings of Ogopogo that are hundreds of years old.

☐ c. The Japanese crew's footage of Ogopogo was not clear.

3. The author tells this story mainly by

☐ a. telling about different people's experiences with Ogopogo.

☐ b. comparing Ogopogo with different monsters around the world.

☐ c. imagining what it is like to see Ogopogo.

Score 4 points for each correct answer.

_____ **Total Score:** Author's Approach

F | Summarizing and Paraphrasing

Put an X in the box next to the correct answer.

1. Which summary says all the important things about the article?

☐ a. The native tribes of Canada may have been the first humans to see Ogopogo, the monster of Lake Okanagan. The monster has several names, including "wicked one," "great beast on the lake," and "lake demon."

☐ b. In 1990 a group came from Japan to take pictures of Ogopogo, a monster that lives in Lake Okanagan. Although they claim they saw the monster, they were not able to take a clear picture of it.

☐ c. Over the years, a monster has been sighted hundreds of times in Lake Okanagan in British Columbia. Though many people believe Ogopogo exists, others don't. No one has taken a clear picture of it.

2. Which sentence means the same thing as the following sentence? "It doesn't show up on any schedule."

☐ a. The monster always shows up late.

☐ b. No one knows exactly when the monster will appear.

☐ c. The monster shows up when people are not expecting it.

Score 4 points for each correct answer.

_____ **Total Score:** Summarizing and Paraphrasing

G | Critical Thinking

Put an X in the box next to the correct answer.

1. Choose the statement below that states a fact.

☐ a. Ogopogo is scarier than the Loch Ness monster.

☐ b. Lake Okanagan is about 80 miles long.

☐ c. Officials in Canada should try harder to catch Ogopogo.

2. Ogopogo and the Loch Ness monster are alike because

☐ a. both have been sighted hundreds of times.

☐ b. both live in British Columbia, Canada.

☐ c. both have been blamed for killing many people.

3. Geoff Tozer and Andy Aikman went from not believing in Ogopogo to believing in it. What was the cause of their change of heart?

☐ a. They found a very large tooth that must have come from the monster.

☐ b. They read a convincing report written by someone who saw the monster.

☐ c. They both saw the monster jump up out of the water.

4. Which paragraphs provide information that supports your answer to question 3?

☐ a. paragraphs 3 and 4

☐ b. paragraphs 5, 6, and 7

☐ c. paragraphs 8 and 9

5. Which lesson about life does this story teach?

☐ a. Some people will believe in a thing whether or not it can be proved that the thing exists.

☐ b. Unless people see something with their own eyes, they will never believe in it.

☐ c. If people see anything scary at a place, no one will ever go near that place again.

Score 4 points for each correct answer.

_____ **Total Score:** Critical Thinking

Enter your score for each activity. Add the scores together. Record your total score on the graph on page 115.

_____ Finding the Main Idea

_____ Recalling Facts

_____ Making Inferences

_____ Using Words

_____ Author's Approach

_____ Summarizing and Paraphrasing

_____ Critical Thinking

_____ **Total Score**

Personal Response

Describe a time when you saw something that you didn't think anyone else would believe in. _____

_____

_____

_____

Self-Assessment

From reading this article, I have learned _____

_____

_____

The Salem Witch Trials

It all began with a group of girls. They often got together to pass the time on long, cold winter afternoons. But one January day, something strange happened. One of the girls—nine-year-old Elizabeth Parris—had some sort of a fit. She ran around the room and rolled on the floor. She screamed and shouted. She hid under a chair.

2   Soon Elizabeth's 11-year-old cousin, Abigail Williams, began to do the same thing. In fact, within a couple of weeks, all the girls in the group starting having fits. The girls' parents were alarmed. They called in a doctor. He could find nothing physically wrong with the girls. He wondered whether their problems had a different cause. He wondered whether witchcraft was to blame.

3   The year was 1692. The girls and their families were part of the Puritan community in Salem, Massachusetts. Puritans believed that evil was all around them. They believed witches could appear at

The sign in this gloomy picture says that this house in Salem, Massachusetts, was a witch house. Salem is where the famous witch trials were held.

any time and cast spells on people. So when they heard that witches might be causing the girls' fits, they wanted to take action.

4   The parents demanded to know who was casting the spells. At first the girls said they did not know. Soon, though, they began to come up with names. The first person they named was Tituba. She was a woman from Barbados who was kept as a slave by the Parris family. Tituba had been with the girls right before they began having fits. She had shown them how people in her home country told fortunes. The girls also named Sarah Good. She was a homeless woman who begged door to door. And they named Sarah Osbourne, an old woman who had not been to church in a year.

5   Town officials rounded up these women. They held public meetings to question them. Sarah Good and Sarah Osbourne denied that they were witches. But each time they did so, the girls flew into fits. The girls fell onto the floor. They rolled around as if in pain and barked like dogs. They claimed they could see the women changing shape and getting ready to attack them.

6   Under these conditions, Tituba acknowledged her guilt. She told the townspeople what they wanted to hear. It was true, she said. She was actually a witch.

Perhaps Tituba did not understand what she was saying. Or maybe she thought people would forgive her if she confessed. In any case, her words stirred people's worst fears. Now they were sure that witches were running loose in Salem. Officials carted Tituba, Sarah Good, and Sarah Osbourne off to jail. Then people looked around for other witches in town.

7   There were. At least that's what the girls said. Over the next few months, the girls pointed their fingers at more people. And others also began naming witches. By May, 200 people had been named as witches. Everyone in town was frightened. No one felt safe. Who would be the next one to be named? Almost every day, more people were taken to jail. Then trials began. Twenty people were found guilty of witchcraft. They were put to death for their crimes.

8   At last the townspeople came to their senses. They began to doubt what the girls were saying. They realized that the so-called witches were just ordinary citizens. Finally, in the spring of 1693, the witch-hunt ended. Those awaiting trial were sent home. And life in Salem calmed down.

9   Still, many questions remained. Even today, 300 years later, no one knows exactly how or why things got so out of control. What caused the girls' fits? What made them say they were under an evil spell? And what made them name certain people as witches?

10   Some people think the girls simply got scared. They had been playing around telling fortunes. This kind of play was not allowed by the Puritans. Maybe the girls made up the story about witches so they would not get in trouble. Or maybe they felt guilty about their games. Perhaps their sense of guilt grew so strong that it made them mentally ill.

11   Some people think the witch trials grew out of larger problems in the town. The Salem Puritans were not one big happy family. They had bitter fights about how to run the town. They also fought over land. Most of those named as witches were enemies of the girls' families. Was this just chance? Or did the girls somehow pick up on their parents' desires to punish certain people in the town?

12   Finally, some scientists think the girls had a real disease. In 1692 Massachusetts towns were struggling to control a fungus in the grain supply. A fungus is a plant that has no leaves or flowers and is not green. Mold is a type of fungus. The fungus in these towns' grain supply was called ergot. Ergot can make people sick. It can make their muscles flinch and their skin crawl. And it can make them see things that are not really there. Could the girls' fits have been caused by ergot? Another disease causes swelling in the brain. Is that what lay behind the girls' fits?

13   We will probably never know the answers to these questions. The girls themselves did not understand what had happened to them. They went on to lead ordinary lives. But for the families of the victims, life would never be the same. The Salem witch trials had shown how frightening and unfair life could be in America's early days.

A | Finding the Main Idea

One statement below tells the main idea of the article. One statement is too general, or too broad. The other statement explains only part of the article; it is too narrow. Label the statements using the following key:

M—Main Idea   B—Too Broad   N—Too Narrow

_____ 1. People are often afraid of things they can't understand. In Salem, Massachusetts, a whole community became frightened when a few girls began to act in unusual ways.

_____ 2. In 1692 and 1693, young girls in Salem, Massachusetts, were having fits. Local women and men were put to death for being witches who put evil spells on the girls. What gave the girls fits is still a mystery.

_____ 3. Scientists are looking for reasons why young girls in Salem, Massachusetts, acted strange. Perhaps a fungus got into their food. The fungus called ergot can make victims' muscles flinch and can make people see things that are not there.

Score 4 points for each correct answer.

_____ **Total Score:** Finding the Main Idea

B | Recalling Facts

How well do you remember the facts in the article? Put an X in the box next to the answer that correctly completes each statement.

1. When a few Salem girls started having fits, people in the community blamed

☐ a. their food.

☐ b. witchcraft.

☐ c. their parents.

2. Tituba was a woman who had shown the girls how to

☐ a. tell fortunes.

☐ b. make dolls.

☐ c. cast magic spells.

3. The Salem community put to death

☐ a. 20 people as witches.

☐ b. 100 people as witches.

☐ c. 200 people as witches.

4. In 1692 the Puritans' grain supply

☐ a. was running low, so the girls were very hungry.

☐ b. was put under a spell by witches.

☐ c. had a fungus that could have made the girls sick.

Score 4 points for each correct answer.

_____ **Total Score:** Recalling Facts

C Making Inferences

When you draw a conclusion that is not directly stated in the text, you are making an inference. Put an X in the box next to the statement that is a correct inference.

1.

☐ a. Most people in Salem had no trouble believing that there were witches among them.

☐ b. All the Puritans were hoping that no one would admit to being a witch.

☐ c. People who had slaves were not allowed in the Puritan community.

2.

☐ a. Confessing to be a witch was the only way to avoid being punished or killed.

☐ b. Puritans never put anyone to death without having certain proof that the person was a witch.

☐ c. People who were named as witches probably doubted that witchcraft was to blame for the strange way the girls acted.

Score 4 points for each correct answer.

_____ Total Score: Making Inferences

D Using Words

Put an X in the box next to the definition below that is closest in meaning to the underlined word.

1. Even though he loved pizza, he was physically unable to eat because his stomach was upset.

☐ a. in a way having to do with the mind
☐ b. in a way having to do with the body
☐ c. in a brave way

2. In the story, the girl used witchcraft to change her enemy into a toad.

☐ a. magical powers that a witch has
☐ b. a fear of witches
☐ c. a means of getting around used by witches

3. After the boy acknowledged that he had broken the window, his mother forgave him and then helped him fix it.

☐ a. admitted having done something
☐ b. denied having done anything wrong
☐ c. became very angry

4. At the end of the trial, the judge decided that the man did steal a car and must go to jail.

☐ a. a time for getting away from everyday life and enjoying oneself
☐ b. the time that someone must spend in jail
☐ c. a time for hearing arguments to decide whether a charge is true

5. Even though her body was weak, she was <u>mentally</u> strong enough to work word games.

☐ a. in a nervous or frightened way
☐ b. in a way having to do with the mind
☐ c. in a happy or joyful way

6. When dogs sleep, sometimes their legs <u>flinch</u>, as if something has startled them.

☐ a. jump up and down
☐ b. move in a jerky way
☐ c. stand very still

Score 4 points for each correct answer.

_____ **Total Score:** Using Words

E | **Author's Approach**

Put an X in the box next to the correct answer.

1. The main purpose of the first paragraph is to

☐ a. describe all the girls who lived in Salem in 1692.
☐ b. show how powerful the Salem witches were.
☐ c. tell how Salem's witchcraft problem began.

2. From the statements below, choose the one that you believe the author would agree with.

☐ a. The people who were called witches did not really cast evils spells on the girls.
☐ b. Only the people who were put to death were really witches.
☐ c. Without a doubt, the girls thought it was fun to call people witches.

3. The author probably wrote this article in order to

☐ a. show how powerful witches can be.
☐ b. tell about a puzzling event from the past.
☐ c. get people to never believe the words of children.

Score 4 points for each correct answer.

_____ **Total Score:** Author's Approach

F | Summarizing and Paraphrasing

Put an X in the box next to the correct answer.

1. Which summary says all the important things about the article?

   ☐ a. The Puritans of Salem, Massachusetts, believed that witches lived in the world. They believed that some people in their own community were witches and were dangerous.

   ☐ b. In 1692, girls in Salem, Massachusetts, began to have fits. The girls named people of the town as witches causing their fits. Twenty people were put to death before the scare ended.

   ☐ c. In January 1692, a girl in Salem, Massachusetts, ran around the room, rolled on the floor, and screamed for no reason. Other girls started having fits too. Maybe their fits were caused by a fungus in their food.

2. Which sentence means the same thing as the following sentence? "The girls pointed their fingers at more and more people."

   ☐ a. The girls could not speak so they just pointed their fingers.

   ☐ b. The girls called more and more people witches.

   ☐ c. During their fits, the girls pointed their fingers.

Score 4 points for each correct answer.

_____ **Total Score:** Summarizing and Paraphrasing

G | Critical Thinking

Put an X in the box next to the correct answer.

1. Choose the statement below that states an opinion.

   ☐ a. Tituba was wrong to have shown the girls how people in her country told fortunes.

   ☐ b. Tituba had come from Barbados and was kept as a slave by the Parris family.

   ☐ c. In 1693 everyone who was waiting in the Salem jail to be tried as a witch was sent home.

2. From information in the article, you can predict that

   ☐ a. everyone will soon agree that the girls had fits because they felt ashamed about playing a game that was not allowed.

   ☐ b. people will wonder for many years about what caused the fits.

   ☐ c. everyone will soon agree that the girls had fits because a fungus made them sick.

3. Tituba and Sarah Good are different because

   ☐ a. only Tituba was called a witch.

   ☐ b. only Sarah Good went to jail.

   ☐ c. only Tituba confessed to being a witch.

4. Which paragraphs provide information that supports your answer to question 3?

   ☐ a. paragraphs 3 and 7

   ☐ b. paragraphs 1, 2, and 3

   ☐ c. paragraphs 4, 5, and 6

5. How is the Salem witchcraft scare an example of something that is still unsolved?

☐ a. No one knows what made the girls act so strange.

☐ b. No one knows how a fungus got into the grain supply.

☐ c. No one knows why the Puritans believed in witchcraft.

Score 4 points for each correct answer.

_____ **Total Score:** Critical Thinking

Enter your score for each activity. Add the scores together. Record your total score on the graph on page 115.

_____ Finding the Main Idea

_____ Recalling Facts

_____ Making Inferences

_____ Using Words

_____ Author's Approach

_____ Summarizing and Paraphrasing

_____ Critical Thinking

_____ **Total Score**

Personal Response

I know the feeling _____

_____

Self-Assessment

Before reading this article, I already knew _____

_____

The Mothman of West Virginia

Something sinister was happening in Point Pleasant, West Virginia. A strange and frightening creature was hanging around the town. No one knew what it was. But from November 1966 to December 1967, more than 100 people saw it. Some thought it was a bird. Some thought it was a man. Some even thought it was an alien. It became known as the Mothman. To this day, no one knows exactly what it was.

2 The trouble began on the night of November 14, 1966. A man named Newell Partridge was sitting at home watching television. All at once, the screen went blank. At the same time, Partridge heard a "loud, whining noise" coming from outside. Grabbing a flashlight, he ran outside to look around. There, next to his barn, stood a scary-looking creature. It was about seven feet tall with red glowing eyes and batlike wings. As Partridge stared at it, a cold chill swept over him, and he felt a growing sense of danger. His dog, Bandit, growled and ran toward the creature, but Partridge himself dashed back inside. He spent the rest of the night with a gun by his side.

3 The next morning, Bandit was gone. The dog was never seen again. All Partridge found were some tracks. "Those tracks were going in a circle, as if the dog had been chasing his tail, though he never did that," said Partridge. "There were no other tracks of any kind."

4 The next night, two young married couples saw the same creature. They were driving in a deserted part of town when it appeared. "It was shaped like a man, but bigger," said Linda Scarberry. "And it had big wings folded against its back." What frightened the couples most of all were its bright red eyes. "They were hypnotic," said Scarberry. "For a minute, we could only stare at it. I couldn't take my eyes off it."

5 When the couples tried to drive off, the creature shot straight into the air and began to follow them. "We were doing 100 miles an hour, and that bird kept right up with us," said Scarberry. "It wasn't even flapping its wings."

6 The frightened couples called the police. One officer later explained why he took their call seriously. "I've known these kids all their lives. They'd never been in any trouble, and they were really scared that night."

The man pictured here is John Keel, the author of The Mothman Prophecies. *It is about the strange creature that terrified the people of Point Pleasant, West Virginia. A movie with the same title was made from the book.*

7   From then on, the creature was seen by more and more people. Two men from the fire department saw it standing at the edge of town. A woman named Connie Carpenter said it chased her as she drove home from church. Ralph Thomas saw it peering into his living room window. And five pilots at a nearby airport saw it fly by at a high speed. All those who saw it described it as scary. They called it "chilling." They said it was "a monster."

8   Meanwhile, dogs were disappearing from town. Some were found dead and cut up in fields. Others vanished completely. Also, people began to have trouble with their radios and TVs. Cars stalled. Phones did not work. And some people reported seeing a strange "man in black" who talked in an odd voice and asked strange questions.

9   For 13 months, the Mothman terrified the people of Point Pleasant. Then something terrible happened. On December 15, 1967, a bridge that led into town fell into the river. The Silver Bridge was 700 feet long. It fell during rush hour. Dozens of cars plunged into the river. Forty-six people died.

10   After this, the Mothman left Point Pleasant. Or at least, no one saw it again. Skeptics say that's because the Mothman was not real. They say folks were now too busy with real problems to let their imaginations keep running wild.

11   Others see it differently. They see a link between the Mothman and the fall of Silver Bridge. Perhaps the Mothman came to Point Pleasant to warn people about the bridge. Or perhaps the creature caused the bridge to fall. One witness did claim to have seen the Mothman on the bridge just before it broke apart. In any case, these people think the Mothman was some kind of an alien creature.

12   Others think the Mothman was an ordinary animal. It might have been a large barn owl. While owls do not grow to seven feet, they do have long wings. These wings make the owls seem bigger than they really are. A sandhill crane is a large bird with red patches on its head. These patches might be mistaken for eyes. Still, owls and cranes both flap their wings when they fly. That is something witnesses say the Mothman did not do.

13   Another theory is that the Mothman was a mutant bird. A mutant animal is one that is very different from its parents. Chemicals had once been stored on land in Point Pleasant. Could that have produced strange birds that grew to unusual sizes and shapes?

14   We will probably never know the whole truth about the Mothman. But people still wonder about it. In 2002 a movie was made. It was called *The Mothman Prophecies*. It was based on the events in Point Pleasant. The movie doesn't solve the mystery, but it does show many of the strange things that happened here just 40 years ago.

A │ Finding the Main Idea

One statement below tells the main idea of the article. One statement is too general, or too broad. The other statement explains only part of the article; it is too narrow. Label the statements using the following key:

M—Main Idea   B—Too Broad   N—Too Narrow

_____ 1. A mysterious winged creature known as the Mothman scared people in Point Pleasant, West Virginia, from November 1966 to December 1967. After a bridge leading to the town collapsed, the Mothman disappeared.

_____ 2. When people see something weird, they usually try to figure out exactly what they saw and why they saw it. Strange sightings and a sad event in West Virginia led people to many different ideas.

_____ 3. The Mothman of West Virginia was a frightening creature that was seen by many people. It looked different to different people. Some say it looked like a bird, and others say it looked like a man. Many say it had glowing red eyes and wide wings.

> Score 4 points for each correct answer.
>
> _____ **Total Score:** Finding the Main Idea

B │ Recalling Facts

How well do you remember the facts in the article? Put an X in the box next to the answer that correctly completes each statement.

1. After Newell Partridge saw the Mothman, he

☐ a. ran into his house and kept his gun by him all night.
☐ b. ran into his house with his dog.
☐ c. drove away as fast as he could.

2. Linda Scarberry told people that the Mothman

☐ a. cried as if it had a broken heart.
☐ b. didn't flap its wings.
☐ c. tried to push her car off the road.

3. The Silver Bridge fell into the river on

☐ a. November 14, 1966.
☐ b. July 4, 1967.
☐ c. December 15, 1967.

4. Just before the bridge fell, a witness saw the Mothman

☐ a. on the bridge.
☐ b. pulling down the poles that held up the bridge.
☐ c. flying over the bridge and laughing.

> Score 4 points for each correct answer.
>
> _____ **Total Score:** Recalling Facts

C | Making Inferences

When you draw a conclusion that is not directly stated in the text, you are making an inference. Put an X in the box next to the statement that is a correct inference.

1.

☐ a. The Mothman appeared only to people who were going to die when the Silver Bridge fell.

☐ b. Newell Partridge's dog was a brave animal.

☐ c. No one in Point Pleasant ever had trouble with a radio, TV, car, or phone before the Mothman appeared.

2.

☐ a. Barn owls and sandhill cranes are birds that are sometimes seen around Point Pleasant.

☐ b. After a while, the people of Point Pleasant enjoyed seeing the Mothman.

☐ c. People who saw the Mothman hardly ever told others that they had seen it.

Score 4 points for each correct answer.

_____ **Total Score:** Making Inferences

D | Using Words

Put an X in the box next to the definition below that is closest in meaning to the underlined word.

1. There was something <u>sinister</u> about the way the frightening old woman stared at us.

☐ a. angry

☐ b. funny

☐ c. evil

2. After the <u>alien</u> landed on Earth, it got out of its ship and looked around at our planet.

☐ a. a light that comes from a distant star

☐ b. a creature from outer space

☐ c. a piece of rock from another planet

3. The swinging watch was soon all I could see or hear. I felt myself slowly falling under its <u>hypnotic</u> spell.

☐ a. able to put someone in a sleeplike state

☐ b. related to gold and jewels

☐ c. able to make someone feel excited and happy

4. The speaker knew that she would need to provide proof to make the <u>skeptics</u> in the audience believe her.

☐ a. people who are not friendly

☐ b. people who are filled with doubt

☐ c. people who will believe almost anything

5. When the woman saw the wet ground, her <u>theory</u> was that it must have rained the night before.

☐ a. belief or idea

☐ b. fear

☐ c. joke

6. The <u>mutant</u> bird could not fly like the other birds.

☐ a. beautiful

☐ b. pleasant

☐ c. different or changed

Score 4 points for each correct answer.

_____ **Total Score:** Using Words

E Author's Approach

Put an X in the box next to the correct answer.

1. The main purpose of the first paragraph is to

☐ a. tell how people described the Mothman.

☐ b. describe the town of Point Pleasant, West Virginia.

☐ c. tell how the Mothman was linked to the collapse of the Silver Bridge.

2. What is the author's purpose in writing this article?

☐ a. to get the reader to watch out for the Mothman

☐ b. to tell about a strange creature who frightened a town

☐ c. to describe what happens when people don't take care of their pets

3. Some people think that the Mothman was a bird, such as an owl or a sandhill crane. Choose the statement below that best explains how the author deals with the opposite point of view.

☐ a. The Mothman couldn't be an owl because it had wide wings, and owls don't have wide wings.

☐ b. The Mothman couldn't be a bird because birds flap their wings when they fly, and the Mothman flew without flapping its wings.

☐ c. The Mothman couldn't be a sandhill crane because it did not look anything like a crane.

Score 4 points for each correct answer.

_____ **Total Score:** Author's Approach

F | Summarizing and Paraphrasing

Put an X in the box next to the correct answer.

1. Which summary says all the important things about the article?

☐ a. Before the fall of the Silver Bridge in 1967, some strange things happened in the nearby town of Point Pleasant, West Virginia. Some dogs disappeared from the town. A few were found cut up in the fields. The radios, TVs, and cars were not working right.

☐ b. The Silver Bridge was a 700-foot bridge that led to Point Pleasant, West Virginia. On December 15, 1967, the bridge fell during rush hour. Many cars fell into the river below. Forty-six people died.

☐ c. The Mothman of West Virginia was a strange creature that was seen by many people for months before a terrible bridge accident in 1967. Some see a link between the Mothman and the fall of the bridge. Others think that the Mothman was just an animal.

2. Which sentence means the same thing as the following sentence? "All those who saw it described it as scary."

☐ a. The people who saw it could be described as scary.
☐ b. All the people who saw it said it was frightening.
☐ c. Everyone who saw it was afraid to describe it.

Score 4 points for each correct answer.

_____ **Total Score:** Summarizing and Paraphrasing

G | Critical Thinking

Put an X in the box next to the correct answer.

1. Choose the statement below that states a fact.

☐ a. The sightings of the Mothman were the scariest things that ever happened in Point Pleasant.
☐ b. Someone should have taken a picture of the Mothman.
☐ c. A 2002 movie called The Mothman Prophecies was based on the events in Point Pleasant.

2. From information in the article, you can predict that

☐ a. everyone will soon agree that the Mothman caused the Silver Bridge to fall.
☐ b. everyone will soon agree that the Mothman was not real.
☐ c. if people see the Mothman again, they may feel nervous about what might happen next.

3. The Mothman and barn owls are different because

☐ a. only the barn owl can fly fast.
☐ b. the Mothman is much bigger than a barn owl.
☐ c. only the Mothman has long wings.

4. In which paragraph did you find the information to answer question 3?

☐ a. paragraph 12
☐ b. paragraph 5
☐ c. paragraph 13

5. How is the story of the Mothman an example of something that is still unsolved?

☐ a. No one knows when the Mothman came to Point Pleasant or when it left the town.

☐ b. There are two mysteries: Was the Mothman real? Was it linked to the fall of the Silver Bridge?

☐ c. No one knows how many people were killed in the collapse of the Silver Bridge.

Score 4 points for each correct answer.

_____ **Total Score:** Critical Thinking

Enter your score for each activity. Add the scores together. Record your total score on the graph on page 115.

_____ Finding the Main Idea

_____ Recalling Facts

_____ Making Inferences

_____ Using Words

_____ Author's Approach

_____ Summarizing and Paraphrasing

_____ Critical Thinking

_____ **Total Score**

Personal Response

A question I would like Linda Scarberry to answer is

" _____ ?"

Self-Assessment

One good question about this article that was not asked would be " _____

_____ ?"

Compare and Contrast

Pick two articles in Unit Three that tell about events that frightened people in the past or still scare them today.
Use information from the articles to fill in this chart.

Title	Name a person or a group that was frightened.	Who or what was doing the scaring?	How did the person or people deal with fear?

Which of these events do you think was or is more frightening? Tell why._____

_____

_____

Comprehension and Critical Thinking Progress Graph

Directions: Write your score for each lesson in the box under the number of the lesson. Then put a small X on the line directly above the number of the lesson and across from the score you earned. Chart your progress by drawing a line to connect the Xs.

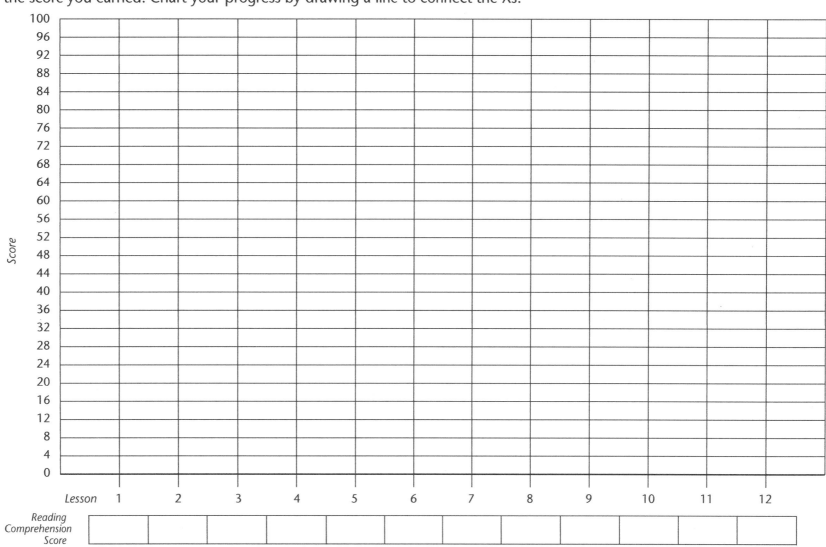

Photo Credits